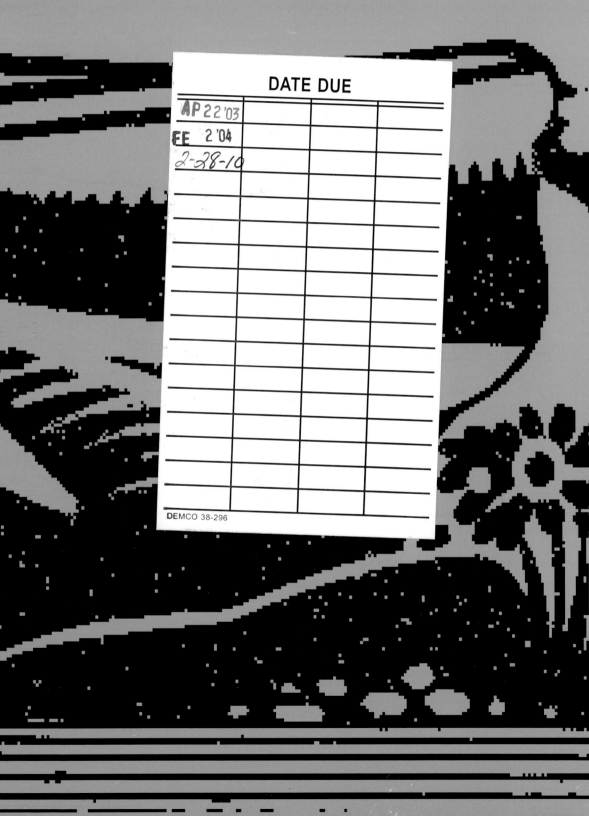

CHILDREN OF THE SLAUGHTER

CHILDREN
OF THE
SLAUGHTER

YOUNG PEOPLE OF THE HOLOCAUST

TED GOTTFRIED

Illustrations by Stephen Alcorn

THE HOLOCAUST
Twenty-First Century Books
Brookfield, Connecticut

Chapter opening illustrations and design by Stephen Alcorn © www.alcorngallery.com

Photographs courtesy of UPI/Corbis-Bettmann: pp. 21, 75; Bilderdienst Süddeutscher Verlag: p. 31; Anne Frank Fonds, Basel/Anne Frank House, Amsterdam/Archive Photos: p. 45; Dokumentationsarchiv des Oesterreichischen Widerstandes/USHMM Photo Archives: p. 51; © Bettmann/Corbis: pp. 66, 84

Library of Congress Cataloging-in-Publication Data
Gottfried, Ted.
Children of the slaughter / Ted Gottfried.
p. cm.
Includes bibliographical references (p.) and index.
ISBN 0-7613-1716-3 (lib. bdg.)
1. Jewish children in the Holocaust—Juvenile literature. 2. Hitler-Jugend—Juvenile literature.
3. Holocaust survivors—Psychology—Juvenile literature. 4. Children of Holocaust survivors—Psychology—Juvenile literature. [1. Holocaust, Jewish (1939-1945) 2. Hitler Youth. 3. Holocaust survivors.] I. Title.
D804.48.G66 2001
940.53'18—dc21   00-030222

Published by Twenty-First Century Books
A Division of The Millbrook Press, Inc.
2 Old New Milford Road
Brookfield, Connecticut 06804
www.millbrookpress.com

For my daughter,
Valerie Gottfried,
and all the world's children
—Peace and Love

ACKNOWLEDGMENTS

I am grateful to personnel of the Judaica Room of the New York Central Research Library, the Mid-Manhattan Library, the Jewish Museum in New York, and the United States Holocaust Memorial Museum in Washington, D.C., as well as those at the central branch of the Queensboro Public Library for their aid in gathering material for this book. Thanks are also due to my friend and fellow writer Kathryn Paulsen for help with research, my friends Janet Bode and Stan Mack, and—with much love—the contribution of my wife, Harriet Gottfried, who—as always—read and critiqued each chapter of this book as it was written.

All contributed, but any shortcomings in the work are mine alone.

—Ted Gottfried

CONTENTS

Europe 1936,
The Eve of World War II

0 — 400 miles

0 — 600 kilometers

NORWEGIAN SEA

N
W — E
S

NORWAY

Oslo

SWEDEN

NORTH SEA

DENMARK

Copenhagen

UNITED KINGDOM

IRELAND
Dublin

NETHERLANDS

Hamburg

Elbe R.

Oder R.

Amsterdam

Berlin

Thames R.
London

BELGIUM

GERMANY

Rhine R.

ATLANTIC OCEAN

Brussels

LUXEMBOURG

Prague

CZECHOSLOVAKIA

Seine R.

Saar

Nuremburg

Paris

Munich

Vienna

FRANCE

Geneva

SWITZERLAND

AUSTRIA

Rhône R.

Venice

Milan

Po R.

Ebro R.

Corsica

ITALY

PORTUGAL

SPAIN

Rome

Tagus R.

Madrid

Sardinia

Lisbon

Algiers

Sicily

Tangier

Gibraltar (British)

Tunis

SPANISH MOROCCO

TUNISIA
(French)

ALGERIA (French)

MOROCCO (French)

Archangel

Dvina R.

FINLAND

Helsinki

tockholm

Leningrad

Volga R.

BALTIC SEA

ESTONIA

Riga

LATVIA

Moscow

Memel

LITHUANIA

UNION OF SOVIET SOCIALIST REPUBLICS

anzig

E. PRUSSIA

Minsk

Vistula R.

Varsaw

Don R.

POLAND

Kiev

Dnieper R.

Volga R.

Budapest

Odessa

HUNGARY

ROMANIA

Belgrade

Bucharest

KINGDOM OF
THE SERBS,
CROATS, &
SLOVENES

Danube R.

BLACK SEA

CASPIAN SEA

BULGARIA

Sofia

ALBANIA

Ankara

TURKEY

GREECE

PERSIA

Athens

Rhodes

Crete

SYRIA (French)

MEDITERRANEAN SEA

Cyprus

Fifty-four people, entire families were brought to the police station
and later taken out of town. One ten-year-old boy returned the next day and
told us what happened. They had been taken to the nearby woods.
At his father's urging, the boy found a moment to slip undetected behind the
trees and hide. He watched from there. The men were given shovels and
made to dig mass graves. Then everyone was shot. Yankel was so strong that
it took seven bullets to kill him. His wife died with her baby daughter in her
arms. As soon as the victims fell, the policemen and some of the spectators
stripped off their clothes before shoving them into the grave. The boy lay
down in a hole and covered himself with leaves.
He stayed there until everybody left. . . . [1]

INTRODUCTION
Witness to Mass Murder

More Than a Million Children Slaughtered

This account of what the ten-year-old boy saw and how he escaped being killed is related by a Holocaust survivor who was himself only sixteen years old at the time he fled the Nazis. They were only two of the Jewish children caught up in the mass murders. According to records in the United States Holocaust Memorial Museum, "1.5 million innocent children . . . were savagely shot, buried alive, burned in the ovens at Auschwitz and other death camps, or otherwise murdered" during those terrible times.[2]

Children made up one quarter of the six million Jews slain by the Nazis before and during World War II. They were victims of a Nazi program to make Europe *Judenrein*—rid of Jews. At first this was done haphazardly, but then the Nazis came up with a program they called the "final solution." Today we call it the Holocaust.

Hitler Youth

The children who were victims of the Holocaust, and those who somehow managed to survive, were not the only children affected by it. In Germany when World War II began in 1939, there were 8,870,000 children—many as young as ten years old—enrolled in the Hitler Youth, the Nazi organization named after the party's leader, Adolf Hitler, formed to ensure future "fighters against the

Jewish enemy."[3] Some 82 percent of eligible German boys and girls belonged to Hitler Youth groups.

Patriotism and German racial superiority were the ideals of the Hitler Youth. These German children were taught to believe the Nazi theory that Germans belonged to the Aryan race and that Aryans were superior to other people. The children were taught that Jews, Gypsies, Slavs, and others were members of inferior races. Soon the children became convinced that these people were less than human. They saw them through Nazi eyes as parasites living off Aryan society, or as roadblocks to Aryan progress. These children grew up to accept the Nazi view that the extermination of these people was necessary to achieve the ordained destiny of the German nation of Aryan supermen.

It followed that the boys of the Hitler Youth were trained for war. The girls were trained to be "strong mothers and obedient wives."[4] Some of the Hitler Youth grew up to take an active part in the slaughter. Some grew up to reject everything that had been drummed into them as members of the Hitler Youth. All were marked by the Holocaust.

Caught in the Middle

Every child in war-torn Europe was touched by the Holocaust as Nazi armies swept over the continent. Some of these children came from families with a tradition of prejudice against Jews. Some of these children lived in places where Jews had been persecuted for centuries. But other children lived in countries where the equality of all people was taken for granted. They came from family backgrounds in which bigotry played no role.

All of these children were drawn into the Holocaust. Some pointed out Jewish victims to the Nazis. Others helped Jewish children hide from the killers. Most simply watched. It seemed to these young witnesses that it was all they could do.

Some of their parents joined with the Nazis in the slaughter of Jews, Gypsies, Communists, members of the rival political parties, and others. Some of these children belonged to families that took in Jewish children and shielded them from the Holocaust. Some became close to Jewish children. Others resented them as family intruders. When the Holocaust came, children reacted in as many different ways as adults did.

Legacy of Survival

It was not just those children who lived through the Holocaust who were scarred by it. The pain and horror has reached forward through the years to affect even children who are decades removed from it. The survivors of the Holocaust, many of them children themselves when the war ended, have passed on their suffering to their own children in a variety of ways.

Some of these children of survivors describe growing up in a climate of fear. Their parents were so anxious that there might be another outbreak of violence against Jews that the children felt they should always be poised to run or fight. Usually, there was no basis in reality for such fears. But the memories of the survivor parents were so strong that their feelings possessed their children as well.

Other children of survivors describe the frustration of not being able to get their parents to discuss what they had gone through in the Holocaust. Many feel they can never measure up to their parents' courage. Some—they find it hard to explain why—feel guilty because of their parents' suffering. A few have trouble accepting the responsibility of keeping the memory of the Holocaust alive, and they resent their parents for expecting them to shoulder it.

Most of the offspring of Holocaust survivors have one thing in common: They have been denied the gift of being as carefree as other children. The burden of history—passed on through their parents—is their legacy.

Legacy of Guilt

The burden of history is also the legacy of another group of children born after the Holocaust ended. These are the sons and daughters and grandchildren of those who participated in carrying out the Holocaust. Some are the offspring of rank-and-file German soldiers who took part in the slaughter. Others are the descendants of high-ranking Nazis. Still others are the children of those in the Nazi-occupied countries who collaborated in killing Jews and who sometimes profited from it.

These children of the guilty must also find a way to deal with their legacy. Some deny the evidence and deny the Holocaust itself. They deny the photographs of death camps taken by the Nazis, the careful concentration-camp records and "Death Books"—records of executions—that were kept and the forty-two volumes of Nuremberg war-crimes trial testimony.[5] Most of all they deny any wrongdoing on the part of their forebears.

Others suspect what their parents may have done, but are not sure. Many aged people refuse to talk about those bad old times. The children, grown now and perhaps with children of their own, live in a state of suspicion and fear of finding out the truth.

Still others do know and are so sickened by the knowledge that they turn away from their parents in disgust. They are ashamed of their parents, grandparents, and older relatives. They are ashamed of their country; ashamed of being German, Hungarian, Polish, French, Ukrainian, Dutch or any of the other nationalities that participated to a lesser or greater extent in the Holocaust. Throughout Europe, even when there was no direct family involvement in the killing, the offspring ask themselves what their parents—or perhaps their grandparents—knew, and what they did—or did not do—about it.

Neither Killers Nor Victims

The Holocaust has a message for all of today's young people: Prejudice is never a reason to kill, or be killed. They—you!—must not grow up to be either killers or victims.

The purpose of this book is to help spread that message. It is a book for young people. It is a book about the children of the Holocaust.

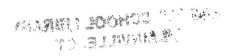

THE FIRST YOUNG VICTIMS

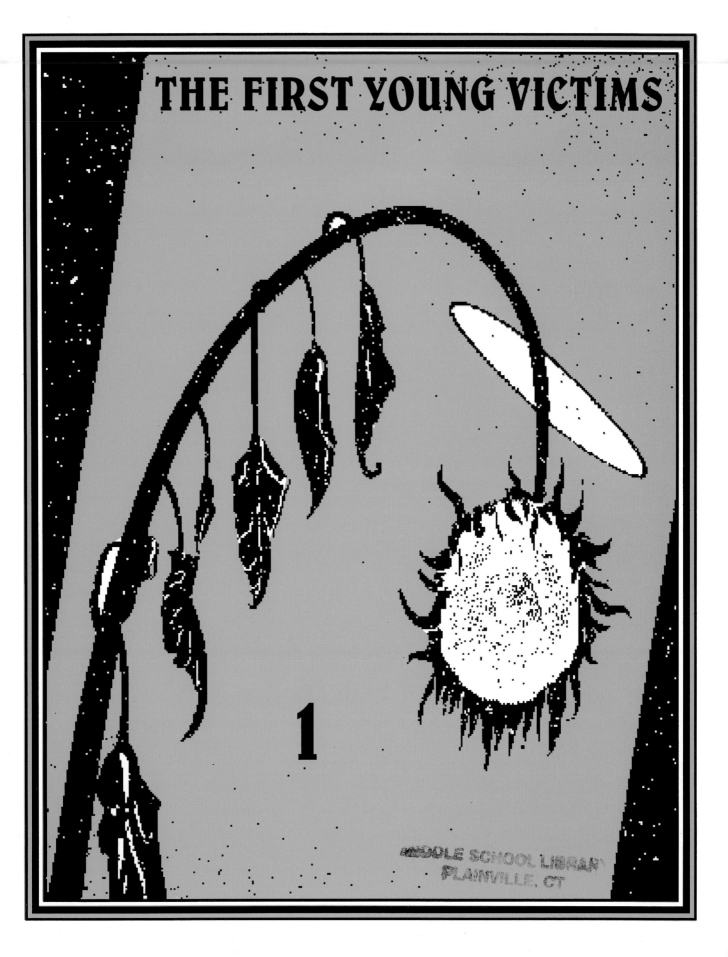

1

ollowing World War I and throughout much of the 1920s, Germany was a nation in turmoil. The economy was in shreds. There was widespread unemployment. By October 1922, money was almost worthless, with four thousand German marks the equal of only one U.S. dollar. (Today, two marks are worth more than one U.S. dollar.) During one month the price of bread had doubled.

The victors in World War I had decreed that defeated Germany pay the cost of the war. This debt—known as reparation—was a burden bitterly resented by the German people. "Bread first, then reparation!" was the protest against the government voiced in the streets.[1] The protest grew when German chancellor Karl Joseph Wirth proposed that Germany declare bankruptcy.

Early Anti-Semites

Earlier in 1922, Walther Rathenau, the German foreign minister who had agreed to war reparations, had been shot by two assassins. Right-wing nationalists were believed responsible. Anti-Semites (Jew haters) had repeatedly accused Rathenau of being a traitor to Germany because he was Jewish.

The Nazis at that time were only one of the anti-Semitic right-wing nationalist parties in Germany, but not yet the main one. They were feared for their vicious street fighting in cities like Berlin and Munich. Their victims were supporters of democracy, trade unionists, left-wingers, and Jews.

Not all Germans approved of Nazi anti-Semitism, but a significant number did. They were not Nazis, but they nevertheless blamed the Jews—many of whom had fought bravely for Germany—for losing the war. It was rumored that Jewish arms manufacturers had supplied inferior weapons at exorbitant prices and that these had cost the lives of German soldiers. It was also said that high interest on government loans by Jewish bankers had robbed Germany of the money needed to win the war. Actually, it was non-Jewish firms (like the major German arms manufacturer, Krupps) which supplied arms to the German military, and the banks were mostly German owned. The few Jewish banks that loaned the government money did so at the same rate as all the other lending institutions. Nevertheless, many government reports from different regions of Germany in the early 1920s reflect "a virulent hatred of Jews that was . . . explosive."[2]

The Young Targets

This hatred was directed at Jewish children as well as grown-ups. It began in small ways. Jewish children were teased. They were called names. Friends who were not Jewish turned away from them. Those who did not turn away told them they were "good Jews," not like other Jews. Jewish children were harassed, taunted, and sometimes beaten.

Some Jewish teenagers found themselves barred from clubs, games, and other extracurricular activities. Their Jewish teachers were forced out of some of their schools, and often the teachers who were left made anti-Semitic remarks. The wearing of the swastika—already a symbol for anti-Semites—had been forbidden in many schools, but it was widely worn in defiance of the prohibition. In upper high school and college classrooms Germany's so-called Jewish problem was the subject of lectures that stressed the danger of Jews to the nation.

Jewish children of all ages were also affected by the expressions of anti-Semitism that were going on around them outside of school. While violence against Jews was not yet organized by the Nazis in the 1920s, it did occur with some frequency. Not all German Jews were discriminated against, but the pressures on those who were victims weighed on their children as well.

The Exodus

The pressures were still bearable when Adolf Hitler came to power in 1933. At that time there were half a million Jews in Germany, or about 1 percent of the German population. Their situation had slowly been growing worse, but then anti-Semitism was a fact of life in many European lands. Countries where it was thought to be less of a problem—although not absent altogether—enforced strict limits on the numbers of Jews that could be admitted. Before 1933 it was not unreasonable to hope that this latest wave of prejudice against Jews in Germany would blow over. Besides, most German Jews considered themselves patriotic Germans and were proud of their fatherland. Why uproot their children to make the costly move to some foreign land where Jews might be no more welcome than in Germany?

That attitude changed in 1933. Over the next five years almost a third of Germany's Jews—150,000—left the country. Between 1938 and the outbreak of World War II in September 1939, an additional 150,000 Jews fled. More than half the Jewish population—300,000 Jews—had already left the country when the beginning of World War II put a stop to any further flight.

Reduced Circumstances

Many of those who left were children. They were of all ages, from infants to adolescents. Often children who had lived comfortably in Germany found that after they left, their families were quite poor. German law forced their parents to leave property behind. There was a limit on the amount of money they could take out of the country, and much of that money had to be used to bribe officials and border guards.

The children arrived in strange lands where they had no friends and little or no spending money. Often they did not speak the language. Sometimes they went hungry. Worst of all, as time passed and the German army conquered Europe, these families, including the children, once again fell into Nazi hands.

The Nazi Hard Line

Jewish children who remained in Germany were affected by the anti-Semitic measures the Nazis took and by the laws they passed. On April 1, 1933, Hitler ordered a boycott against Jewish businesses. With Nazi government encouragement, anti-Jewish signs sprang up throughout Germany decreeing: "JEWS NOT WANTED HERE!" and "ENTRY FORBIDDEN TO JEWS" and so forth.[3] The effect of such signs on Jewish children was devastating.

That same month laws were passed barring Jews from civil-service jobs, from serving as jurors, and from working at state institutions as doctors, dentists, or dental assistants. In May a law was passed excluding Jewish professors and lecturers from universities. In September and October, Jews were barred from the fields of art, literature, theater, and film. When the government took over all German newspapers, Jews were forbidden to run them or work on them in any capacity.

In the future Jewish children would, of course, be barred from pursuing careers in these areas. Some laws targeted them directly. One spelled out strict limitations on the number of Jewish children who could enroll in German public schools.

The Nuremberg Laws

There was a lull in anti-Semitic activity toward the end of 1935. It ended with the so-called Nuremberg Laws decreed by Hitler that year. The first of these, the Law for the Protection of German Blood and German Honor, "prohibited marriage and sexual relations between Germans and Jews, forbade Jews to display the national flag, [and] prohibited Jews from employing female citizens of German or kindred blood under forty-five years of age."[4] It was followed by the Reich Citizenship Law, which said that Jews were subjects, not citizens, of

Germany. This meant that Jews could not vote or hold office. A while later the law was amended to define someone as a Jew "if they (1) belonged to a Jewish religious community; (2) were married to a Jew; (3) were offspring of marriages contracted with Jews after June 15, 1935; or (4) were born out of wedlock to Jews."[5] Again, children with Jewish blood had been specifically targeted.

All together, some four hundred laws and decrees affecting Jews were passed.[6] Also, a four-year plan was drawn up by the Nazi government and the army generals for wartime. As one historian explains, "In the case of war, the Four-Year Plan envisioned the expropriation of all Jewish property in Germany."[7] To help identify Jews, the Nazis also ordered that "all male Jews must assume the given name of Israel, while all female Jews had to take the given name of Sarah."[8] This included children, some of whom were young enough to be thoroughly confused by the name changes.

The Boy Who Struck Back

Over the next couple of years, things got worse. German villages took measures to become "Jew-free." Jews "could be arrested without due process and imprisoned in concentration camps." Bewildered children were suddenly left fatherless, and sometimes without mothers. Jews' "property could be seized and confiscated for the flimsiest of reasons. They had no legal recourse."[9]

In November 1938 one Jew, a disturbed teenager attending school in Paris, struck back. His name was Herschel Grynszpan, and he was seventeen years old. His parents were among the fifty thousand Polish Jews who had been living in Germany. When life became unbearable under the Nazis and they tried to leave, the Polish government refused to let them return to Poland. The Gestapo (Nazi secret police) then began rounding up the Polish Jews and putting them in camps near the German-Polish border. The Jews were held there in "appalling conditions."[10]

According to German-born historian Klaus P. Fischer, "Young Grynszpan wanted to send a message of protest to the world [by performing a] desperate

Herschel Grynszpan, shortly after his arrest in Paris in November 1938

deed."[11] On November 7, 1938, he shot an official of the German embassy in Paris. The assassination was like a match lighting the dynamite fuse of German anti-Semitism.

Kristallnacht

Two days after the assassination, Nazi ruler Adolf Hitler approved "spontaneous" actions targeting Jews. The storm troopers (official hoodlums of the Nazi Party), Hitler said, "should be allowed to have a fling."[12] Meanwhile, in small towns across Germany, mobs goaded by storm troopers "went into action, setting fire to the local synagogues, destroying Jewish businesses and homes, and manhandling Jews."[13]

The madness spread over all of Germany. So many windows of shops and homes were broken that the streets in Jewish neighborhoods were covered with broken glass. The fragments gave the terror its name—*Kristallnacht*, "the Night of Broken Glass."

Jewish institutions and Jewish-owned factories were burned to the ground. More than seven thousand Jewish businesses were destroyed. Thousands of Jews—men, women, and children—were driven from their homes and tormented, or beaten in the streets. More than one hundred Jews were killed.

The Nazis blamed *Kristallnacht* on the Jews. Jewish-owned businesses were forbidden to reopen. Plans were drawn up to confiscate Jewish business establishments and factories. The Nazi government issued a "Decree on Eliminating the Jews From German Economic Life."

All Jewish children were expelled from German public schools. They could only stay home with their parents, many of whom were scrambling to get out of Germany. Some made it. But approximately 200,000 people of all ages did not get out of Germany. Most of the children among them eventually ended up being killed in the gas chambers of Nazi death camps.

HITLER

YOUTH

2

Adolf Hitler, you are our great Führer. Thy name makes the enemy tremble. Thy Third Reich comes, thy will alone is law upon earth. Let us hear daily thy voice and order us by thy leadership, for we will obey to the end and even with our lives. We praise thee! Heil Hitler![1]

—"Prayer" recited by members of the Hitler Youth

uring the last week of April 1945, only days before the end of World War II, the Battle of Berlin was fought by the Germans against the invading Allied armies. Among the defenders of the capital city of Germany were five thousand members of the Hitler Youth. Most of them were fifteen and sixteen years old. A few were as young as twelve years old. Only five hundred of the five thousand were left alive when the battle was over. The rest had fulfilled their vow to "obey to the end and even with our lives."

Their Final Battle

They were the youngest of the Hitler Youth. After the war the organization was disbanded. By 1945 those who had started out as members of the Hitler Youth in the 1920s were more than thirty years old. They had fought in the battles of World War II; they had rounded up Jews and executed them; they had manned the gas chambers and the ovens in the death camps.

From childhood, they had been well trained to obey orders, no matter how inhumane. The discipline that made this possible had been drummed into them from the time they were ten years old. As adults they acted out the lessons learned as children of the Hitler Youth.

Future Storm Troopers

The *Hitler Jugend, Bund Deutscher Arbeiter-Jugend* (Hitler Youth, League of German Workers' Youth) began with a notice in the Nazi party newspaper in 1922. Earlier, party leader Adolf Hitler had announced the formation of a Nazi youth group. If the party was to have a future, he realized, it must attract young people.

At that time the party was best known for the fighting and bullying done by its military wing. These street brawlers were known as "Brownshirts" because of the uniforms they wore.[2] Their official name was *Sturmabteilung* (storm troopers). Usually this was shortened to SA.

The Nazi party's first call for young people stated bluntly the purpose of Hitler Youth: to ensure that there would be future recruits for the SA. A rigorous program of body building, sports, hiking, and lectures stressing Nazi ideals and anti-Jewish policies was designed to shape the storm troopers of tomorrow.

Swastika Bullies

At first only boys were recruited by the Nazi youth group. It was not acceptable that young German girls should be trained as future storm troopers. The Hitler Youth was still exclusively male when it was officially established as a unit of the Nazi party in July 1926.

By that time Hitler had served a prison term for leading a failed revolt against the democratic government of the Weimar Republic, established following World War I, and had written *Mein Kampf* (*My Struggle*), which defined Nazism and became the party bible. The Nazi party was becoming well known. Its membership was growing. Many Germans who were not members agreed with Hitler's aggressive racist, anti-Jewish views and with his plans to rearm Germany and extend its borders.

The boys who joined the Hitler Youth were formed into bands that were attached to adult SA units. They wore brown storm-trooper shirts and swastika armbands. They handed out propaganda leaflets and worked to recruit other boys to the Hitler Youth. Sometimes they would gang up on other youngsters—foreigners, Gypsies, but most of all Jews—and beat them up.

"To Die for the Fatherland . . ."

There were meetings twice a week, with lectures on racial purity. There were regular hiking trips on the weekends where the boys were deliberately pushed to the limit of their endurance. There were summer camps. .

"At the camps were a lot of games," a man who had been a member of the Hitler Youth as a ten year old recalled. "The games were most of the time oriented toward paramilitary training." He remembered that "it was soldiering. It was exercises on how to conceal yourself in the country, how to attack enemies. . . . It just was a promotion of the patriotic spirit."[3]

How did this "patriotic spirit" make him feel?

"To die for the Fatherland sounded really great," he remembered.[4]

Faithful, Pure, and German

A girls' organization was formed in 1927. In July 1930 it became one of the two main branches of the Hitler Youth. (The boys' division was the other.) Each of the branches had two subdivisions, defined as follows:

1. The German Young Folk (*Deutsches Jungvolk,* or DJ) for boys aged ten to fourteen. A young boy in this group was usually referred to as a *Pimpf* (cub).
2. The Hitler Youth (*Hitler Jugend*, or HJ) for boys aged fifteen to eighteen.
3. The League of Young Girls (*Jungmädelbund*, or JM) for girls aged ten to fourteen.
4. The League of German Girls *(Bund Deutscher Mädel*, or BDM) for girls aged fifteen to eighteen.[5]

The motto for girls of the Hitler Youth was Be Faithful, Be Pure, Be German! They were taught from *Mein Kampf* that a German woman "is a subject and only becomes a citizen when she marries." They learned that "the goal of female education must invariably be the future mother."[6]

For the boys of the Hitler Youth, the motto was Live Faithfully, Fight Bravely, and Die Laughing![7]

Baldur von Schirach's Master Plan

In 1933, when Hitler came to power in Germany, the membership of the Hitler Youth totaled 107,956. The young people's group was headed by Baldur von Schirach, who had taken it over when he was only twenty-four years old. When he assumed command the Hitler Youth had been plagued by mismanagement, careless record keeping, and failures in collecting dues and camp fees. Von Schirach, a fanatic Nazi and Jew hater with a baby face, had straightened out the mess, tightened the organizational structure, and come up with a program for the future that would make the Hitler Youth a centerpiece of Hitler's Germany.

It was a simple plan. He would bring all German youth movements into the Hitler Youth and make them conform to its program and principles. Eventually there would be only one young people's movement in Germany—the Hitler Youth.

By the end of 1933, the majority of German youth groups had become part of the Hitler Youth. Only Catholic groups, which had strong beliefs of their own that differed from Nazi beliefs, held out against being part of von Schirach's organization. Jewish youth groups, of course, were excluded anyway.

The State Becomes the Parent

Three years later, on December 1, 1936, a law was passed making the Hitler Youth "a supreme Reich authority *(Reichsbehorde)* directly responsible to

Hitler." It proclaimed that "all German Young People, apart from being educated at home and at school, will be educated in the Hitler Youth physically, intellectually, and morally."[8] It ordered that this education be under the control of Baldur von Schirach.

On March 25, 1939, five months before World War II began, a second law was passed. It made membership in the Hitler Youth compulsory. Hitler Youth—almost nine million strong—was now the largest youth organization in the world.

Parents who did not register their children in the Hitler Youth faced fines and imprisonment. Some recognized that the purpose of the Hitler Youth was to wean their children away from them and transfer their loyalty to the state, but their hands were tied. "Young people," one German historian has written, "were deceived by a smoke screen of youthful idealism."[9] Their parents could only listen as they sang such Hitler Youth songs as "Holy Fatherland," or chanted slogans like "Hitler is Germany and Germany is Hitler."[10]

The Junior Gestapo

In 1938 a subgroup was created within the Hitler Youth. Called *Streifendienst* (Patrol Service), these chosen young people were assigned to monitor the activities and conversations of other children and to report back to the police on improper activities or "treasonous" views. They were a sort of junior version of the Gestapo—the secret police who made sure that German civilians obeyed Nazi laws and conformed to Nazi dogma.

The *Streifendienst* would report children who saluted improperly, sang forbidden songs, or violated the Hitler Youth curfews. Young people were reported for smoking, drinking, or behaving in a rowdy fashion in poolrooms or dance halls.

Members of the *Streifendienst* were responsible for teaching younger children and new members of the Hitler Youth the Nazi theories of German racial superiority. It was their job to stamp out behavior and speech that was disloyal, or that deviated from the doctrines and rules of the Hitler Youth.

Parents at Risk

Reinhard Heydrich, in charge of national security, found a wider use for the *Streifendienst* in the summer of 1939. He ordered that training sessions be held for these elite members of the Hitler Youth to teach them the most sophisticated techniques of spying. They were taught that their duty was to report to Nazi authorities any *adult* activities or conversations that were disloyal. This meant targeting neighbors, teachers, religious leaders, and even parents.

The training was effective. There were cases of youths turning in their parents to the authorities. One boy, Walter Hess, reported his father for making anti-Hitler remarks. His father was punished. Walter was rewarded with a promotion in the Hitler Youth. Other boys were assigned to churches to report on any anti-Nazi content in sermons.

Telling on adults was an activity practiced by all the Hitler Youth, not just the *Streifendienst*. Older boys and girls handed out forms to younger children and saw to it that they were filled out. The forms required the young children to report any adult who had said or done anything that might interfere with the mission of the Hitler Youth.

Of course, the adults with whom these children most often came into contact were their parents. It follows that their parents were the adults most at risk. In this way the Nazis used the younger German children as a weapon to keep the children's parents in line.

Nazi Morality

These parents had reason to be critical of the Hitler Youth program. According to one German historian, the Hitler Youth produced a "generation of young Germans intolerably loutish and belligerent."[11] It cannot have been easy to live with such children. To be judged by them must often have seemed outrageous.

There were other problems as well. Where the boys were segregated from the girls in the Hitler Youth camps there were frequent reports of male homosexual activity. This was a problem because homosexual behavior was a crime in Nazi Germany. It could be punished by castration or even death.

Where the sexes were not segregated, there was a different problem. Many of the teenage girls of the BDM came home pregnant from the Hitler Youth camps. It did the parents no good to protest, try to protect, or discipline their daughters. The girls had been brainwashed.

William L. Shirer, in his history *The Rise and Fall of the Third Reich,* reports attending lectures given by women leaders to young BDM girls that stressed "the moral and patriotic duty of bearing children for Hitler's Reich—within wedlock if possible, but without it if necessary."[12] The only shame was if the baby's father was not 100 percent German.

The Memory of Power

During World War II, after Germany invaded the Soviet Union, the penalty for suggesting that Germany should surrender was death. A child who overheard such a remark at the dinner table held the offending parent's life in his or her hands. The child's first loyalty was to Hitler.

What was it that claimed such extreme loyalty? Why was the Hitler Youth so fanatical? What was it that attracted the children and held them through deliberate physical hardship, alienation from their families, harsh restrictions, and unending discipline? What did they get out of the Hitler Youth? Here, in their own words, is how some former members explained it:

"... there will always be the memory of unsurpassed power, the intoxication of fanfares and flags proclaiming our new age."[13]

"I wanted to escape from my childish, narrow life and I wanted to attach myself to something that was great and fundamental."[14]

"... in the Hitler Youth, you did learn discipline."[15]

"Exercises, lectures in history, political lectures, the purity of the Aryan race ..."[16]

"We dreamed then of a strong Germany . . . and Hitler promised to fulfill this dream for us. . . . we followed him blindly. . . . we had forfeited our freedom of conscience."[17]

Hitler Youth Goes to War

That forfeit began in 1936 when hundreds of seventeen-year-old boys from the Hitler Youth were recruited for the SS Death's Head troops that guarded the concentration camps in Germany. Over the following years the cream of the Hitler Youth was drawn into volunteering for SS service. By mid 1940 there were 60,000 Hitler Youth, aged seventeen and up, serving with the SS. Some of them, and some of those who followed, served as guards and performed technical and administrative functions in the death camps of Eastern Europe. The Hitler Youth was well represented among those who carried out the Holocaust.

When World War II began, the Hitler Youth boys aged ten and older were given rifle practice and training in military maneuvers. In 1942 special military training camps were set up for older boys. They were put through three weeks of the most rigorous training. The need for discipline and unquestioning obedience was drilled into the boys.

Meanwhile, BDM girls were being sent to Poland to help new German farmers work the land that had been taken from the Poles. They were part of a policy known as the "Germanization" of Europe.[18] The idea was to populate occupied Poland with pure-blooded Germans. Many of the Poles displaced under this program ended up in slave labor camps, some of them in Germany itself.

Work was hard for the BDM girls, and the hours were long. The teenagers had to deal with inexperienced German settlers who had little or no farming experience. They had to face the hostility of Poles in the towns and villages. They had to nurse the sick and work in the fields. And they had the responsibility of seeing that Nazi rules and doctrine were not violated. (One rule forbade hiding Jews.)

Wounded Hitler Youth fighters stand at attention during a ceremony in 1943. The Nazis prohibited this photograph from appearing in newspapers.

What was their reward? If they stayed long enough they could look forward to marriage with a pure-blooded German man, the bearing of pure-blooded German children, and the carrying out of the Nazi goal of *Lebensraum* (room to live)—Hitler's policy of seizing land for German use. The girls were being programmed for breeding even as they helped to enforce Nazi policy.

Sacrificing the Young

Starting in 1941, younger German children, both boys and girls, also were used in the war effort. They performed low-skilled jobs in the post office and in railway yards. They were government messengers. The majority worked on German farms. In 1942, two million boys and girls helped to harvest food to feed the nation and the troops.

By 1943, however, the tide of war was turning against the Nazis. German soldiers were dying by the tens of thousands. There were almost 200,000 German casualties in the Battle of Stalingrad, Russia, alone. The army desperately needed more soldiers.

The Hitler Youth programs were intensified. Now ten year olds were trained to use machine guns and bazookas. They were taught how to fight tanks with live hand grenades. Sixteen year olds were signed up for active duty. By 1944 the German army was taking boys as young as fourteen.

A Hitler Youth tank division was formed and fought against Americans in France. It went on to fight in Belgium in the Battle of the Bulge, and later in Hungary. Its casualties were very heavy. Barely trained fifteen year olds led by sixteen year olds died in great numbers.

The Pride and the Shame

When the fatherland was invaded by Allied troops, the Nazis drafted all fifteen year olds to defend German soil. Officer training centered on this group. But they were both inexperienced and outnumbered in battle. Tens of thousands of young boys were killed as the Russian army advanced into Germany.

Advancing from the west, the American army took prisoners of war as young as eight years old. The Americans even executed two saboteurs aged seventeen and sixteen. They were members of a Nazi unit called *Werewolf*—young boys and girls trained to be spies and to commit acts of espionage.

In the last days of the war the defense of Berlin meant the final slaughter for the Hitler Youth. Once they had sung, "Today Germany belongs to us, and tomorrow the whole world."[19] They had believed it with all their hearts. Now there was nothing left to believe. The *Werewolf* recruits had been the pride of the Hitler Youth. In the end, they were its victims.

THE LOSS OF CHILDHOOD

3

On the night of November 10, 1938, in Vienna, Austria, where I was born, the Germans suddenly smashed all the windows in my parents' clothing store. . . . German soldiers were dragging Jews into the street and taking them away on trucks. . . . I was eight at this time, and my brother, Kurt, was four. . . . I remember becoming especially frightened when the twenty-one-year-old janitor of our building came to our door dressed in a Nazi uniform and told us the apartment was now his.[1]

— Ruth Bachner, Holocaust survivor

All across Europe children like Ruth Bachner were stunned, bewildered, angry, and afraid as the Holocaust began for them. In Austria anti-Semitism had been growing as the Nazis came to power in Germany. When German troops marched into Austria in March 1938, Austrian Nazis took over the government. Laws persecuting Jews were followed by actions against them.

Two months later the Hungarian parliament passed anti-Jewish laws. Italy passed laws against Jews in November 1938. In Romania, the Iron Guard, a government-approved Nazilike military organization, began harshly persecuting Jews in 1937 and 1938. Nazi anti-Semitism spread to Czechoslovakia in 1938 and 1939 when German troops occupied that country.

The Spreading Plague

With the official start of World War II, anti-Semitism was unleashed all across Europe. In many places it was already a part of the culture. In Belgian cities, for example, before the Germans came, there were signs: "JEWS DON'T APPLY HERE FOR APARTMENTS."[2] Within two years after the 1940 occupation of Belgium, Jewish children were taken out of public schools, often made to pin yellow stars to their clothing indicating their status as Jews, and ganged up on by other children.

Stolen Childhood

Restrictions were applied to Jewish children in all the countries the Nazis occupied, including the Netherlands, Belgium, France, Norway, Greece, and Yugoslavia. They were barred from schools, playgrounds, movie theaters, swimming pools, and parks. In France the Nazis decreed that "it is forbidden for Jews from the age of six upwards to appear in public without wearing the yellow star."[3]

The king of Denmark, a Christian, himself put on a yellow star to show support for the Jews, and in that country the anti-Semitic laws were mostly not enforced. But Denmark—along with Bulgaria—was an exception. In most occupied territories, there were enough people with anti-Jewish attitudes to make the lives of Jewish children miserable.

"I, who was always the first in my class, was just thrown out of high school," remembers Lydia Gasman-Csato, who was a Jewish teenager in Romania during those times. Her best friend "sent me a letter saying that she couldn't be friends with me because I came from a cursed race." Gasman-Csato sums up the emotions she felt with such words as "humiliation" and "lack of dignity."[4]

The Paris Roundup

In the beginning, in the countries of Central and Western Europe, the hurt for Jewish children was psychological and sometimes physical, but usually not life threatening. That soon changed. When the Nazis occupied a country, their goal was to make it *Judenrein*. The first step was to round up the Jews, including the children.

A major roundup took place in German-occupied Paris on a night in mid-July 1942. Acting for the Nazis, the French police assigned 888 arrest teams—9,000 men—to seize 27,388 Jews. Neighborhoods where Jews lived were sealed off, and at four in the morning, squads of French police banged on doors and forcibly entered Jewish homes.

Apartment houses swarmed with police. Jewish families were forced out of their homes and into the streets. One terrified ten-year-old girl fled from the police and jumped to her death from a sixth-floor window. As dawn broke, bewildered Jewish children of all ages—some only infants—found themselves being forced to march with their parents toward an unknown destination.

The Vélodrome d'Hiver

More than four thousand children and three thousand adults were herded to the *Vélodrome d'Hiver*, an indoor sports stadium. What followed was chaos. There were ten toilets for more than seven thousand people. There was no water for either washing or drinking. For five days the children and adults had neither food nor water. The July heat was intense, sickness spread, and the stench was unbearable.

It had already been decided that Jewish adults were to be deported from France to camps in the East. But what to do with the children? While it was true that the German Nazis controlled Paris, they were concerned that the French Vichy dictatorship, established with the consent of the Germans to rule unoccupied France, might object to deporting Jewish children.

However, far from objecting, Vice Premier Pierre Laval of Vichy was one step ahead of the Nazis in Paris. His attitude was made clear in a telegram from Nazi headquarters in Paris to Berlin:

> *Laval has proposed that children below the age of sixteen be included in the deportation of Jewish families from the free zone [Vichy]. The fate of Jewish children in the occupied zone does not interest him.*[5]

"I Have Nothing Left"

The parents were deported first. The children—some of the smallest ones torn from their mothers' arms—remained behind at the *Vélodrome d'Hiver*. A Red

Cross worker smuggled out a note from a seven year old to the *concierge* (janitor, or caretaker) of the small apartment house in which the child had lived:

Madame la concierge,
  I am writing to you because I have nobody else. Last week Papa was deported. Mama has been deported. I have lost my purse. I have nothing left.[6]

Within two weeks after the note was written, the children were shipped out of Paris to camps in the East. Between 70,000 and 80,000 French Jews perished in the Holocaust. Of the children who were deported, "no child ever found his or her way back to France."[7]

The "Righteous Gentiles"

In Paris, as in all of Europe, there were children who were not caught in the Nazi net. Seeing what was coming, many Jewish parents acted to protect their children. Some had them baptized in the Christian faith and made arrangements with Christian families to shield them through the war. Some placed their children—even infants—in Catholic orphanages.

Organizations were formed to save the children. Christians active in this effort became known and honored as "righteous Gentiles" (non-Jews).[8] They forged birth certificates and passports, established a sort of underground railway system in which Jewish children were passed from house to house until they could either be transported out of the country or hidden safely. Protestant clergymen, Catholic priests, and foreign diplomats all took part in these rescue networks. But the majority of those who shielded the Jewish children were women.

Nevertheless, these valiant rescuers were strangers to the children. The young people were confused. There were no familiar faces. They didn't know whom to trust. Before becoming separated from their parents, they had been warned about so many things.

If their family name was a Jewish name, they were warned never to reveal it. One survivor who spent her childhood in hiding recalls that "I didn't remember anymore what my real name was. I only dreamt about it at night. When I woke up in the morning, I wouldn't remember again. I knew that I had a different name, but it was so important for me to forget it that I actually did completely forget it."[9]

The Price of Refuge

Some of those who took the children offered shelter, but little else. They did not nurture them or love them. Some used them as servants. Some abused them.

In Hungary the father of eight-year-old Gabor Kalman paid a man to take his son and hide him from the Nazis. Gabor Kalman remembers: "The man who took me home brags to the neighbors that he may be a Fascist, but he is no fool. He is hiding a Jewish boy, just in case Hitler will not win the war."[10]

There were older city children hidden on farms who were treated as field hands. They rose before dawn and worked in the fields until after dusk. A sparse meal and a few hours of sleep later, they were back in the fields again. It was the price they paid for not being turned over to the Nazis.

Some paid a different kind of price. Another survivor remembers how when she was an adolescent, the man who was sheltering her "embraced me and took me close . . . and I was suddenly afraid. . . . It happened two more times . . . he always came upstairs, and he never did it when his wife was there."[11]

"They Loved Me So Much . . ."

Most of these children, however, were not mistreated. Some remember their foster families with love and affection. Max Arian, for instance, was taken in by a Dutch miner's family with two older children. "They asked for a little Jewish baby girl," he remembers, "and they got a little boy of two-and-a-half years with a drippy nose and with a doll of rags. . . . I think they loved me from the first moment. And I had a beautiful time. . . . I was so much a member of the family. They loved me so much; I felt so warm and safe."[12]

The families who took in the Jewish children risked their lives. The children knew this and were grateful. At the same time, they wanted to be with their own real families. There were unavoidable resentments and frictions.

There were also pressures for the children who were not separated from their families, but who went into hiding with them. Sometimes this meant living in crowded quarters under difficult circumstances. Always it meant giving up the freedom to move beyond the hiding place and enduring the constant fear of discovery. A Dutch girl named Anne Frank kept a diary of what that life was like.

The Diary of Anne Frank

Actually, Anne Frank was born in Frankfurt, Germany. In 1933, when she was four years old, the Nazis came to power and the Frank family fled Germany. They settled in Amsterdam, the Netherlands. In 1940 the Germans occupied the Netherlands.

Because she was Jewish, under Nazi rule eleven-year-old Anne was no longer allowed to go to the school she had been attending. Her father was forbidden to run his business. In February 1941 the Nazis began rounding up Amsterdam Jews. On July 5, 1942, Anne's sixteen-year-old sister, Margot, was ordered to report for deportation. At that point the entire Frank family went into hiding.

Anne, her parents, and her sister, Margot, moved into a "secret *annexe*" in the attic of a combination warehouse and office building.[13] Here they were joined by the Van Daans—father, mother, and fifteen-year-old son, Peter. An elderly Jewish dentist also joined them in hiding.

These eight people lived together in close quarters and with the danger of discovery for two years. During those two years, Anne never left the attic. She was cut off from the outside world—from friends; from the freedom to take a

Anne Frank

walk, go skating, or ride a bike; from flowers and trees, sun and wind, songbirds and butterflies. During that time, when Anne was thirteen and fourteen years old, she kept a diary that would one day be read by people all over the world.

Anne's diary details the daily frictions among the eight people in the attic. It speaks of the lack of privacy grating on everyone's nerves—particularly those of an adolescent girl. It describes the difficulties of smuggling in enough food to feed everyone. She writes of listening with a pounding heart as the Gestapo searched the area just beyond their secret hiding place.

"If God Lets Me Live . . ."

Despite the terror, the hardships, and the conflicts, Anne was always optimistic. When she and Peter Van Daan fell in love, her account was both heartbreaking and inspirational. On April 17, 1944, Anne wrote as follows:

> *Do you think that Daddy and Mummy would approve of my sitting and kissing a boy on a divan—a boy of seventeen and a half and a girl of just under fifteen? I don't really think they would, but I must rely on myself over this. It is so quiet and peaceful to lie in his arms and to dream . . . will Peter be content to leave it at this? . . . Why, then, should we who love each other remain apart? Why should we wait until we've reached a suitable age? Why should we bother?* [14]

Anne's situation, her awakening sexual feelings, and her confusion about how far she should let them take her, came to an abrupt end on August 4, 1944. The Gestapo had found out about the secret annex. Anne and all the others hiding there were caught.

"If God lets me live," Anne had written in her diary a few months before, *". . . I shall work in the world and for mankind!"* [15]

THE
KILLING
GROUND
4

nne Frank was taken from Gestapo headquarters in Amsterdam to a reception camp at Westerbork. From there she was sent to Auschwitz in Poland. Auschwitz was a death camp, but Anne was young and healthy and able to work, so she was not killed. In October 1944, Anne was shipped to the Belsen camp in Germany. A typhus epidemic had broken out there. In March of 1945, fifteen-year-old Anne died. Less than two months later, the war ended.

Death Trains for Toddlers

Anne had been part of the last shipment of a thousand Jews to leave Holland. Other transports had left previously from all the Nazi-occupied countries of Europe. Hundreds of thousands of people were jammed into boxcars—stifling in summer, unheated and freezing in winter—for days at a time, with no food, water, toilet facilities, or room to sit down.

Many of those locked in the boxcars were children. Some were infants. Twenty percent of the so-called death-train Jews from Belgium and 12 percent of those from France were under the age of fifteen.

A Red Cross worker in Paris described the scene when children who had been separated from their parents were loaded into the boxcars. "The freight cars had no foot boards, and many of the children were too small to step up. The bigger ones climbed in first and helped pull in the smaller ones. . . . They did not want to leave and began to sob. . . . I remember little Jacquet, aged five and especially endearing. Begging for my help he called out, 'I want to get down . . . .' The door of the wagon was closed and padlocked, but he still stuck his hand out through a crack between two planks; his fingers moved; he continued to cry out . . . ." The train guard "gave that hand a blow."[1]

The Hero Mother

Many children, as well as adults, suffocated or were trampled to death in the boxcars. Passengers who survived were unloaded at railroad yards outside the death camps. Those who were fit to work were separated from those sent immediately to the gas chambers. The doomed group included people who were ill or crippled, old people, and pregnant women, as well as children.

Esther Geizhals-Zucker remembers that when she arrived at Auschwitz as a fourteen year old, her family saw a four-year-old girl separated from her father. "My mother . . . took this child by the hand and she kept her, wouldn't let go of her. . . . Everything happened very rapidly. . . . When he [the Nazi official] asked my mother if this was her child and she nodded yes, he sent her to the left. My brother being only twelve at the time, he sent to the left, and me he motioned to the right. . . .

"I wanted to run to my mother. . . . A Jewish woman who worked there caught me in the middle and said, in Polish, 'Don't you dare move from here!' Because she knew that if I was on the other side I would go to the gas chamber. . . . That was the last time I saw my mother. . . . a hero: a woman who would not let a four-year-old child go by herself."[2]

Other children had preceded fourteen-year-old Esther Geizhals-Zucker to the various camp factories where slave laborers were worked to the point of exhaustion and then were murdered in the gas chambers. Among them were those who had survived earlier, less methodical Nazi slaughters. These had begun with the Nazi invasion of Poland in September 1939.

The Forced Marches

At that time there were about 3.35 million Jews in Poland. The poorest lived in ghettos (all-Jewish city neighborhoods) and some lived in *shtetlach* (small country villages populated by Jews), but most lived among the Poles. There was anti-Semitism in Poland, but the Jewish children went to school with the Polish children, played with them, and even made friends with them.

That changed when the Nazis came. Jews were then rounded up. Jewish children, along with their parents, had to endure forced marches to ghettos and work camps during the brutally cold winter of 1939–1940, when temperatures reached forty degrees below zero. Many people became ill. The children who could not keep up were shot by their Nazi captors. Other children watched as their parents were killed.

The children who survived the marches arrived in places where tuberculosis and typhus epidemics were raging. One such destination was the Lublin District, where fifty thousand Jews—a good many of them children—toiled as slave laborers. The Lublin District later became a center for the mass killing of Jews.

The "Final Solution"

The majority of Poland's Jews were not caught in the first roundups. Then, in July 1941, *Reichmarshall* Hermann Göring issued the order for the "final solution of the Jewish question."[3] The killing of Polish Jews and their children and of Jews and their children who had fled to Poland from other countries under Nazi control would no longer be done randomly. Execution squads would sweep across occupied Poland and into Latvia, Lithuania, Estonia, the Ukraine, and Russia with the specific assignment of murdering Jews "without regard to age or sex."[4]

At first the killings were carried out with pistols, rifles, and machine guns. After able-bodied Jewish men were separated from their families and sent to

Taken secretly at a station in Poland, this photograph shows a train that along with its occupants, was headed to the death camp at Treblinka.

work camps, women and children were marched off to be shot. Some of this killing was done face-to-face, one-on-one; some was done by squads firing at groups.

In the ghettos the killing was haphazard. One Jewish survivor was sixteen years old when he witnessed a German soldier throw a baby from a window high up in an apartment building. Another describes the morning after a killing orgy in which her family was murdered: "The next morning, as I walked through the streets, I had to step over bodies."[5]

The Killing Vans

To make the killings more efficient, around the end of 1941 those in charge decided to use vans. Carbon monoxide from the exhaust pipes was pumped into the vans' enclosed compartments. Up to 150 people at a time were locked in the compartments—more if small children were among them.

The vans moved from killing site to killing site. There was no time to get rid of the corpses. This presented a health problem, as well as a problem in maintaining relations with the local people in occupied areas. The locals were understandably upset by heaps of corpses near their villages.

Questions of how to kill large groups of people efficiently led to a conference at Wannsee, just outside of Berlin, in January 1942. High-ranking Nazis discussed plans for mass killing facilities. The result was modernized death camps with chambers for gassing large numbers of people and ovens for disposing of the bodies.

The Warsaw Ghetto

By this time most of the Jews left alive in Poland who had not been shipped to work camps had been herded into ghettos. In Warsaw, one of Europe's largest ghettos, the prewar population was 160,000. After the Nazi roundup, there were roughly 400,000 people crowded into the Warsaw ghetto. Among them were many children who had become separated from their parents.

The ghetto was walled off from the rest of the city. There were "27,000 apartments with an average of two and one-half rooms each" that housed roughly five to six people per room.[6] Many of the ghetto children, however, did not live indoors.

Chaim Kaplan, a Warsaw teacher, described the plight of the children after the Nazis closed their schools. He wrote: "Thousands of them are out on the street because there are no schools for them. They remain untutored, uneducated, and above all unfed."[7]

"The most fearful sight is that of the freezing children," wrote Emmanuel Ringelblum in November 1941. "Little children with bare feet, bare knees, and torn clothing, stand dumbly in the street weeping. . . . I heard a tot of three or four yammering. The child will probably be found frozen to death tomorrow morning. . . ."[8]

Between July and October 1942, 310,322 Jews were transported out of the Warsaw ghetto to the death camps. In January 1943, 6,500 more Jews were shipped out. In April 1943 the Germans moved in to clear out the Jews who remained there.

They were met by armed resistance. Young Jews led the way in pitched battles against the German army. Snipers, children among them, fired on the Germans from the rooftops. The final action had been scheduled to take three days. It took four weeks of intensive fighting against young and untrained Jews with nothing to lose but their lives to finally clear out the ghetto.

The Death Camps

Most of the Jewish children who were shipped from the Warsaw ghetto and other locations throughout Europe to the death camps were killed upon arrival. Some of the sturdier ones were put to work in one of the many factories that were established close to the camps to take advantage of the prisoners' labor. Some children worked in the camp kitchens or cleaned the prisoners' barracks. Some children worked in the stables where the Nazi officers kept their horses, and some dug ditches. Near the entrance to the gas chambers, one "little Jewish boy of three or four years of age . . . was made to hand out bits of string with which the victims had to tie their shoes together."[9] All of these children were worked to the point of exhaustion, and almost all eventually were killed. Their stories are terrible. Their days were marked by one ghastly horror after another. They lived with the stench of the ovens, with the risk of a bullet from a Nazi who shot children for sport with a telescopic rifle, and with the fear of growing too weak to work and being gassed.

One French Jewish boy, Georges-Andre Kohn, was sent to Auschwitz when he was eleven years old. His case was reconstructed through documents and evidence presented at the Nuremberg Trials for war crimes after it was all over. In the bitterly cold November of 1944, Georges-Andre was assigned to work outdoors, wheeling a cart loaded with trash or wood. He became weak and feared that if he could no longer work he would be sent to the gas chamber.

He wasn't. Instead, he was shipped with twenty other children to the concentration camp of Neuengamme, just outside Hamburg, Germany. When they arrived there, Georges-Andre and the other children were put in the camp's hospital wing, not to rest but for another purpose.

Medical Research

They were fed well. They did not have to work. In contrast to Auschwitz, their quarters were heated. They were to be the subjects of a series of medical experiments.

Georges-Andre was injected with germs from a variety of diseases, including tuberculosis. Incisions were made on his body. He became so weak that he had to be carried to and from the examining rooms.

At the end of April 1945, Germany was on the verge of losing the war, and it was decided to conceal the evidence of the experiments. The children were told that they were being transferred to another camp. Instead they were driven to an empty school. Georges-Andre was given an injection of morphine, as were the other children. Then they were made to undress. Naked, they were hanged. The youngest victim was five years old.

By now, the Soviet, American, and British armies were liberating the death camps. The daily horror was over for those Jewish children still left alive. Many had lost their parents, their brothers and sisters, their families. All had lost their childhood.

5

THE SURVIVORS

The police, and Polish soldiers, stood around and laughed
as stones were being thrown at me. Some Poles said
"Look. There's still a Jew alive."[1]

—Fifteen-year-old concentration-camp
survivor Solly Irving describes his
return to his hometown of
Ryki, Poland, after the war.

Of the 1.6 million Jewish children under the age of sixteen who lived in the warring countries of Europe before World War II, only 175,000—11 percent—survived. They were hidden by non-Jewish families. Forged papers were obtained for them. They hid out in forests and sparsely settled farmlands where they foraged for food. Some who had been caught in the large-scale Nazi roundups of Jews were strong enough to work in the various concentration-camp factories run by the Nazis. Some survived the concentration camps and were fortunate enough to find one or both parents, or some other relative, still alive and to be reunited with them. Some who were not so fortunate had entered the camps as children and now left them as adolescents, or adults, to strike out on their own.

There were those, however, who were still children and who survived to find that their parents were dead and that they were alone. They were orphans among the 715,000 Jews that Allied forces liberated from the concentration camps. Initially, these children "were entirely on their own, lone survivors in a chaotic world, surrounded by ruin and desolation. . . ."[2]

A Chaotic World

There was great confusion everywhere at the end of the war. Many of the children fled the concentration camps as soon as they could. Often they had no destination in mind. They just wanted to get away, and so they joined the hordes of refugees—Christians as well as Jews from every country—who jam-packed the roads.

Many of the children, however, were too weak to leave the camps. They were ill and on the verge of starvation. At first there was no transportation to move them. They stayed in the camps to receive food and medical treatment.

Killed With Kindness

As a young boy, Moshe Avital, who would later become a doctor, was held in nine different concentration camps. He was at Buchenwald when it was liberated on April 12, 1945. "The American soldiers did not know how to do enough for us," he remembered. "However, they made a terrible mistake by giving rich food to very sick people who had not tasted a morsel of food for a long time. . . . Our stomachs were not accustomed to it. As a result, thousands died."[3] The "rich food" was mostly candy bars the soldiers carried in their pockets.

There were also epidemics of disease at the various camps. At the time that Belsen was liberated, a typhus epidemic was killing about a thousand people a day. The Theresienstadt camp had to be quarantined because of typhus. Other diseases—tuberculosis and pneumonia in particular—struck young people who were already suffering from starvation.

The effort to save the children took time to organize. Jewish groups all over the world participated. The most prominent were the Joint Distribution Committee, based in the United States, and the Palestine Jewish Brigade.

The Wanderers

The first job that faced these groups was to bring some kind of order to the chaos. Jewish orphans were wandering with other homeless children in the streets of war-torn cities throughout Europe. They were on the road, strewn over the countryside, seeking family members who often no longer existed. They were in displaced person (DP) camps, hospitals, and orphanages.

The majority of the Jewish orphans were not among those liberated from the concentration camps. Instead, they were children who had lived out the war with Christian families, or who had been placed in monasteries or Christian orphanages. Some had escaped from the camps or the ghettos, and had lived in the woods, foraging for themselves. They had no way of knowing whether their parents were alive or dead, or where they might be. They wandered and they hoped, often in vain.

Nor were Jewish children the only ones orphaned in the war. Children of every nationality had lost one parent or both to the battlefield, the bombings, the sieges of cities, and the extreme food shortages and disease, which were by-products of the conflict. Children of all nations and religions were rounded up along with adults and placed in DP camps.

The DP Camps

In these camps, by order of American general Dwight Eisenhower, the Jews—including the children—were grouped according to their former nationalities. Eisenhower did not want to segregate them by religion because he felt that would "somehow lend credence to Hitler's racial theories."[4] The sad result, however, was that Jewish DP children once again found themselves a persecuted minority because of widespread anti-Semitism among non-Jewish victims of the Nazis.

As early as August 1945, a report to U.S. president Harry Truman stated that "Jews were treated virtually as war prisoners, subjected to intimidation by non-Jewish DPs and to the confinement, uniforms, and food rations of prisoners."[5] Jewish children of all ages were jeered at and beaten by other refugee children.

Conditions improved when General Eisenhower toured the camps and ordered reforms. The Jewish children were housed separately. Their food rations were increased. Rehabilitation programs were started. Efforts to resettle the orphaned children slowly began.

Postwar Anti-Semitism

Some Jewish children were already trying to resettle themselves. Fifteen-year-old Ben Helegott and his twelve-year-old cousin made their way back to Poland. They were seized by Polish military officers who cursed them as Jews, robbed them, and threatened them with death. Their native land could never again be their home.

There was still prejudice against Jews in most of the countries of Europe. Eva Grant was five years old when the war ended. She had spent virtually her entire childhood in the Theresienstadt concentration camp. After being liberated she was sent to a school in her native Czechoslovakia. She remembers: "There were anti-Semitic children at school. . . . They sang songs about dirty Jews." Later, when Eva relocated to Israel, she learned that "being Jewish was okay in Israel."[6]

Eleanor Roosevelt Prevails

Sometimes the problem was not anti-Semitism, but a lack of interest. In her book *Children With a Star*, Deborah Dwork of the Yale University Child Study Center recorded that "returning children received little sympathy from their neighbors, and . . . indifference from their national governments." The concern was with rebuilding war-torn countries. Jewish children "were not part of the mainstream."[7]

European governments after the war were either democratic or dominated by the Soviet Union. Either way, they officially discarded Nazi racism and anti-Semitism. They declared "that all citizens were the same and were to be treated equally."[8]

The problem was that Jewish children were unlike other war victims. Their experience as Jews—torn from their parents, witness to unspeakable horrors, never knowing whom to trust—made them different. Many were terrified at the idea of being returned to the places they had fled.

In early 1946 the problem of relocation was the subject of bitter debate at one of the committees of the newly formed United Nations (UN). The Soviets argued that displaced persons—presumably including children—who refused to go back to their homelands were "traitors, war criminals, or collaborators." Actually, they considered them anti-Communists and potential political troublemakers. UN delegate Eleanor Roosevelt, widow of President Franklin Delano Roosevelt, led the fight against forcing people to "go home" and "probably bé killed."[9] The UN Assembly was persuaded by her and decided that refugees would have a choice about where to resettle.

A Bitter Welcome

The decision came too late for 150,000 Polish Jews—most of them families with children—who had fled to Russia from Poland when the Nazis invaded. Before the UN ruling could take effect, they were sent back to Poland. They were not welcomed.

Some Poles had taken over Jewish property, and now they did not want to give it back. In July 1946, in a town called Kielce, a series of anti-Semitic riots killed sixty-one Jews and wounded sixty others. Riots targeting Jews followed in other towns throughout Eastern Europe.

As a result, 120,000 Jewish refugees fled to the DP camps controlled by the U.S. Army in Germany and Austria. By the end of 1946, there were 250,000 Jewish refugees crowded into these camps. Many of the refugees were children; some of these were orphans, and some were members of families. This sudden increase interfered with relocation efforts. The Jewish children—particularly the orphans—were trapped in a holding pattern with hopes of rescue fading fast.

Blocked by Quotas

A great many of these children were fed and given clothing and medical treatment by the American-Jewish Joint Distribution Committee. This organization ran 114 schools and kindergartens, 74 religious schools, and 24 clinics, hospitals, and orphanages in the DP camps of Germany and Austria. They also cared for DPs in France, as well as provided aid to refugee Jews outside the camps. By the summer of 1947, the committee was dealing with approximately 750,000 Jewish adults and children.

Most of these people did not want to go back to their homelands because they feared for their safety. Efforts were made to find relatives, particularly in the United States, who would take in the Jewish orphans. Likewise, children with one or both parents still alive were eager to go with them to the United States.

Their way was blocked by U.S. immigration law quotas. These were based on prewar population figures. The Jewish children were classified according to their homelands. The quota for Germany—where there were few Jews left—was high, but low for the Eastern European countries that most of the Jewish refugees had fled. The result was that by the autumn of 1946, almost a year and a half after the war ended, only 2,400 Jewish DPs had been admitted to the United States.

The Zionist Role

If they could not go to America, most Jewish DPs wanted to go to Palestine—the territory that included the nation we know today as Israel. The children in the camps, like the adults, were influenced by the Zionists. The Zionists were struggling to establish a Jewish homeland in Palestine. They brought food, clothing, and medical supplies and—most of all—the hope of a country that Jewish children might call their own.

During the postwar period, Palestine was a land populated by Arabs, Christians, and Jews. It was ruled by the British who had once promised that

Jews could emigrate freely to Palestine. After the war, however, the British went back on their promise. With so many Jewish refugees, the United States had come to favor mass resettling in Palestine, but both the British and the Arab nations opposed it.

The Zionists bought small ships and began smuggling Jewish refugees into Palestine illegally. The British set up a naval blockade to stop them. Shiploads of refugees with many children among them were seized by the British, and these Jews were put into internment camps on Cyprus, an island in the Mediterranean Sea.

The Exodus

In July 1947 the ship *Exodus* set out for Palestine from the coast of France with four thousand Jewish DPs aboard. Teenagers, younger children, and infants were part of the human cargo. The British intercepted the *Exodus* and tried to board her. The Jews fought them off but were finally overwhelmed. All four thousand Jews were shipped back to Germany.

The incident served to turn the tide of world opinion, and eventually the British agreed to the United Nations' partition of Palestine and the creation of a Jewish state—Israel. A war between Jews and Arabs immediately followed. The Jews won that war.

Jewish child refugees now had a realistic hope for a new life. They had a country to turn to, a land to fight for, and Jewish leaders to follow. Jewish children everywhere no longer saw themselves as potential victims.

Vengeance and Forgiveness

For the Jewish children who lived through the Holocaust, however, new hope did not mean forgetting. As the years went by and they became adults, they could not help but think about what they had been through. Whatever meaning they found, though, was different for each of them.

Children are herded from the *Exodus* in July 1947.

Richard lived through the Holocaust as a child. As an adult, he says, "I have lost trust in humanity."[10] Another survivor who went through Auschwitz as a child remembers that "I lost my mother, father, and brother. . . . The problem is how to live with it and not go crazy."[11] George, a German Jew who was born in 1934 and lived through the Holocaust, cannot forgive. "I hate the Germans for what happened," he says.[12]

Jack Rubinfeld reached a very different conclusion. He was sixteen years old and starving when his German guards fled from the advancing American army at the end of the war. Some days later he found two loaves of bread in an abandoned railway car. He remembers that "a German woman with two small children approached me asking for food. She said that they had not eaten for a day. I looked around, ashamed to let my friends see. I broke off half a loaf and gave it to them."[13]

He thought a lot about that incident. Much later when he was a grown man, he said it had been "a decisive moment, showing my inability to seek vengeance."[14] And that, too, was a child's legacy of the Holocaust.

A
LEGACY
OF
GENOCIDE

6

When you live after the fact, you feel an impotent rage. You ask, even though you know the answer: Why didn't anyone do something to stop it? . . . One of my fantasies . . . is getting my hands on a Nazi. . . . I would like to torture him and mutilate him. It scares me when I have thoughts like that. . . . In normal circumstances I can't imagine myself doing violence to any other human being.[1]

—Robert Eli Rubinstein,
twenty-nine-year-old son
of Holocaust survivors

The Holocaust continues to affect many people who had no direct involvement in it. Its pain and horror reach forward through the years to affect young people who are decades removed from the tragedy. The first to be affected were the offspring of the survivors, the children born soon after the Holocaust, who were its immediate heirs.

Their parents were not like the parents of other children, and that made them feel set apart from other children. Some of that first post-Holocaust generation, like Robert Rubinstein who is quoted at the beginning of this chapter, were filled with a hatred they could neither feel comfortable with nor release. Others grew up with feelings of unexplained dread, and with feelings of being guarded against disasters too terrible to discuss.

Survivors' Secrets

Some children knew that their parents were survivors, but the knowledge was incomplete. "I thought I knew a lot about their experiences," related a daughter of survivors. "But only recently, I found out my father had a family before the war. They kept it a secret from me. . . . When I asked my father why he didn't tell me, he said my mother didn't want to think about it. . . . It was very shocking for me to find out he had a wife and son. . . . It's made me wonder what else they have kept from me."[2]

What Madeleine Albright Didn't Know

Many children of survivors "experienced their parents as troubled, secretive, and incapable of talking about the past."[3] Others were simply stonewalled so effectively by their parents that they never knew their parents' history. "Even now," reported *The New York Times* in 1997, "50 years after the war's end, thousands of adults in Europe, the United States, and Russia continue to discover that their origins are not what they had been told."[4]

One such startling revelation came to light with the appointment in 1997 of Madeleine K. Albright as secretary of state of the United States. She is the first woman ever to serve in this position. Shortly before she was sworn in, Albright received documents uncovered by a *Washington Post* reporter that showed that her parents had never told her certain key facts about her background. The full tragedy of her family's involvement in the Holocaust had been kept from her.

Although born Jewish, Madeleine Albright was baptized and raised as a Catholic. She was a toddler just before the war when her family fled the Nazi invasion of Czechoslovakia and took refuge in London. She grew up knowing nothing of her Jewish roots and believing that her family was Catholic. This was not unusual. "Every single day," according to the national director of the B'nai B'rith Anti-Defamation League, "Jews surface who thought they were Catholics all their life."[5]

In the late 1930s and early 1940s, Jewish children were being killed. For Jewish parents to convert their children to Catholicism was a way of ensuring their survival. With pogroms (violence against Jews) occurring after the war ended, there was good reason to continue the deception. By not telling a child of his or her Jewish heritage, there would be no chance of the child letting this information slip and risking anti-Semitic violence.

Protecting the Children

So it was that Madeleine Albright was raised as a Catholic. She never knew that her parents were Jews. Nor did she know that her grandfather and grand-mother had both died in the gas chambers and that an uncle, aunt, and cousin had also been killed by the Nazis. Why was she not told the truth in later years when she was an adult?

The wounds of the Holocaust were deep and painful, and many children of survivors report on how difficult it was for their parents to discuss even those facts that directly related to their children. There was also the fear of presenting an otherwise happy and well-adjusted offspring with what would have been an identity crisis.

The shock of learning that she had lived a lie has not soured Ms. Albright's feelings about her parents. "I think my father and mother were the bravest people alive," she said upon learning the truth. "They dealt with the most difficult decision anyone could make. I am incredibly grateful to them, and beyond measure."[6]

Eating and Starving

When the past was not hidden by their parents, there were many problems for the children of survivors. Their parents had lived through the death camps to find themselves persecuted in DP camps and facing incredible difficulties to emigrate to the United States or to Israel. They were not quick to give up the techniques of survival that had worked for them. Their children were cherished perhaps more than other children, but they were often brought up to regard survival skills as a primary concern.

Some grew up learning that a little money can make the difference between living and dying. Some were taught that a neighbor's smile may hide a heart filled with bigotry and hatred. Some learned—either directly or by example—

that to survive one must be hard and unemotional. The feeding pattern for the children of many survivors was to eat as much as possible while food was available, the unspoken message being that starvation might be just around the corner.

Indeed, food is an issue frequently mentioned by children of Holocaust survivors. Mostly, there are memories of having been overfed as young children. Sometimes, however, it worked out differently. One daughter of survivors spent long years suffering from anorexia nervosa—an obsessive desire to lose weight by starving oneself. "I wasn't worthy to prosper," was the way she put it. "Becoming anorectic and getting my body under control was a self-imposed concentration camp."[7]

Survivor Guilt

This person felt guilty for the horrors her parents had gone through before she was even born. It is a form of what psychiatrists call "survivor guilt," a condition often found among the children of Holocaust victims.

Survivor guilt is usually associated with soldiers in battle. It refers to the feelings experienced in the wake of a common battlefield occurrence: A soldier is beside a comrade who is killed, and his first reaction is relief that he himself is still alive. But his buddy is dead, and he then feels guilty for his joy in being alive. Sometimes that feeling of guilt can stay with him for a very long time. Sometimes it lasts a lifetime.

When the children of Holocaust victims realize what their parents have been through, their first reaction may be a feeling of relief that they will not themselves have to experience such suffering. Then they feel guilty because they thought of themselves rather than the anguish of their parents. When they are children, what they are feeling is hard for them to understand. Nor does it always become clear when they reach adulthood.

Concentration camp survivors display the numbers with which the Nazis branded them. These survivors, now refugees, had just arrived in New York in 1946.

Living up to Auschwitz

This mix of feelings is examined by cartoonist Art Spiegelman in *Maus: A Survivor's Tale, I* and *II*, illustrated books focusing on his relationship with his father, a survivor of Auschwitz. "I somehow wish I had been in Auschwitz with my parents," Spiegelman writes, "so I could really know what they lived through."[8] It is a fantasy shared by many of the children of survivors.

"Every boy, when he's little, looks up to his father," observes the psychiatric counselor in Spiegelman's drawings. The response by the adult Spiegelman is that this sounds true, but he has trouble remembering. Then, however, he blurts out a feeling echoed by other children of Holocaust survivors: "No matter what I accomplish, it doesn't seem like much compared to surviving Auschwitz."[9]

Spiegelman's father, who is dead now, was a difficult parent. "I hated helping him around the house," Spiegelman writes. "He loved showing off how handy he was and proving that anything I did was all wrong. He made me completely neurotic about fixing stuff."[10]

"Existing for the Past"

The experiences Spiegelman describes are similar to those of other children of survivors. Dr. Vivian Rakoff, a psychiatrist who has treated many of these children, found that often patients' problems came from trying to live up to the perfection their parents demanded of them. The parents passed along the most unreal expectations, as if their children could somehow make it all right that the parents had lived when so many others had died.

Such survivor demands were often impossible for the children to meet. Too often what was really passed along was the full strength of the parents' survivor guilt. In one case, the burden was too much for an eighteen-year-old boy. He attempted suicide, but failed. "I have been existing *for the past* . . ." his suicide note read, "and as of tonight I hope I shall cease to exist."[11]

His case is an extreme example. More commonly, the survivor parents were overprotective, and their children grew up fearful to some degree. Others stressed the need to be strong and taught their children to be aggressive. Sometimes, though, the children turned that lesson aside, and sought peace and order in their lives, but felt guilty for rejecting their parents' advice.

A Legacy of Dreadful Fantasies

When they were still very young, some of these children tried to make sense out of what their parents had been through. Helen Epstein, author of *Children of the Holocaust*, began asking questions of her mother before she was five years old. "Who put the number on your arm?" she asked about the tattoo that all concentration camp inmates had been forced to wear. "Why? Did it hurt?"[12]

Her parents were honest with her. They told her that all four of her grandparents had been killed by the Nazis. Her father had also lost a fiancée and two brothers. Her mother had lost a husband. Her mother and father, both death-camp survivors, had met after the war and married. She was born soon afterward. Always, her parents tried to answer her questions.

Helen Epstein grew up as an American child with an interest in baseball and the music of the time. "But when my mother took me to Carnegie Hall," she remembers, "I would often imagine a group of men in black coats bursting into the auditorium and shooting everybody dead." She recalls that "when I rode the subways at rush hour, I pretended the trains were going to Auschwitz."[13]

Helen Epstein could not tell her parents about these fantasies. "My parents had a stake in my 'normalcy,'" she has written. Nor could she discuss it with her friends. Other children of survivors whom she met later "recall the same sense of isolation."[14]

Support From One Another

For many years there was no organized effort to bring together the children of Holocaust victims so that they might lend support to one another. Then, in November 1979, almost thirty-five years after the war, the First International Conference of Children of Holocaust Survivors was held in New York City.

Those who attended drew from each other the strength to discuss the effect of their legacy. For some it was the first time they had ever spoken about the Holocaust except in terms of their parents. Many felt for the first time that they were not alone.

Currently, there are many support groups for those with a Holocaust burden. Many years ago, their pain was put into words by Holocaust scholar Shaman Davidson and reported in *Time* magazine under the heading "Legacy of Terror." "The trauma of the Nazi concentration camps," he said, "is re-experienced in the lives of the children and even the grandchildren of camp survivors."[15]

They are the second and third—and by now possibly the fourth—generation of Holocaust victims. Today, however, they are dealing with their pain and coming to terms with it. The past may never be dead for them, but the future is very much alive.

Who can imagine a thirteen-year-old girl stupid enough never to have heard of the horrors of concentration camps and naive enough to believe everything her parents told her? The first shock was to find out what had happened; the second, to find out that my father had played a part in it. Of course I knew that there had been concentration camps and that six million Jews had been murdered. We'd been told about it in school. But I had also been told fairy tales in school . . . who could believe that the baker next door or the English teacher or that nice policeman . . . participated in the murders during the war? And one's own father![1]

—A German woman describes
how she felt as a young girl when
she learned that her father had
worked in a concentration camp.

er name was Anna. She was born in 1947, two years after the war ended, in Munich, Germany. It was 1960 when she learned the truth about her father. Her description of how it made her feel was first published in 1987 in Germany. It is part of a book called *Born Guilty: Children of Nazi Families* by Peter Sichrovsky, which appeared in the United States the following year.

By that time, like Anna, most of the children of Germans who had been in the war were in their forties. Today a third generation—grandchildren—are college age or older. But they, like their parents, are faced with questions of responsibility and guilt.

The Question of Collective Guilt

The hardest question has to do with collective guilt. If, as a matter of policy, the Nazi government that was elected by the German people systematically murdered six million Jews, then are the German people guilty *as a nation*? Does each adult German alive during those years share in the guilt?

Was the genocide the result of a flaw in the German character? Is that defect still there today, lurking in the hearts of Germans born decades after the Holocaust? For how many generations must the blame be borne?

Yes, there was a history of anti-Semitism in Germany before the Nazis came to power. There is still bigotry in Germany today; vandalism in Jewish cemeteries and violence by skinheads against minority populations demonstrate that. But does that mean that all young Germans must share the guilt for all atrocities, past and present?

"The Deeds of Their Fathers"

Many people—Germans, Jews, and others—do not believe in the idea of collective guilt for Germans. They point out that bigotry and violence today are problems in many countries, including the United States, not just Germany. Looking at the Holocaust, they find that Austrians, Poles, Ukrainians, Czechs, Hungarians, French, Dutch, and others took part in the slaughter. If non-Nazi Germans are guilty because they turned their backs, then so are those in other countries who did not want to know—countries such as Great Britain and the United States.

Former West German chancellor Helmut Kohl addressed these concerns during a visit to Israel in 1984. "The young German generation does not regard Germany's history as a burden," he said, "but as a challenge for the future. They are prepared to shoulder their responsibility. But they refuse to acknowledge a collective guilt for the deeds of their fathers."[2]

For young Germans, however, it is often not that simple. For them it is not just a matter of what Germany did. It is much more personal than that. It is what their own parents or grandparents did, what defect in their character made them do it, and how that flaw may have been passed on to them. The issue for them is more than just guilt. It is that there may be a monster inside them capable of unspeakable acts.

The Burden of Knowing

The fear was felt most deeply by the first generation born of Nazi parents. Often the deeds of their parents were hidden from them, but not always. Sometimes the knowledge was too much to bear.

According to Rudolf, son of a major Nazi war criminal who escaped prosecution, "the dreams are worst of all."[3] Rudolf was born in 1950, and by 1960, when he was ten years old, he and his parents had moved four times to elude Nazi hunters. Once, when his father was drunk, he told Rudolf how terrible it had been to have to shoot Jewish children with a handgun because subordinates had aimed their automatic weapons over their heads to avoid killing them.

When Rudolf describes one of his dreams, it sounds startlingly like some of the fantasies of children of Jewish Holocaust survivors: "They tear me from my bed, drag me through the room, down the stairs, and push me into a car. . . . We arrive at a house I don't recognize. I'm pushed down the stairs into a cellar, they rip my pajamas off and push me into a room. The door closes behind me. . . . There are showerheads on the wall, and through the openings something streams out with a soft hiss, like air from a defective bicycle tire. I have trouble breathing; I think I'm choking. I rush to the door, try to open it, rattle it, scream, my eyes are burning. Then I wake up."[4]

Rudolf acknowledged his parents' guilt and hated them for what they had done. After they died, he took their guilt for his own. He has thought about suicide. "At times," he says today, "I wish it were all over."[5]

Not to Blame?

Sometimes the guilt about the action of Nazi parents is so intense that it causes an opposite reaction in the second generation of children. Throughout her teens, Stefanie has had nothing but contempt for the guilt her father feels about the things done by her grandfather. She wants no part of his guilt, and so she denies the legacy of the Holocaust.

Stefanie's father was twelve years old when his father was hanged as a war criminal. When he realized the horror of his father's crimes, he turned to religion for help in dealing with the knowledge. He and his wife brought up both Stefanie and her older sister to face the facts of the Holocaust and of their grand-

A woman accused of collaborating with the Nazis when they occupied Laval, France, is made to wear a swastika and is paraded through the streets of the town.

father's role in it. Atoning was a responsibility that he passed on to them. Stefanie's sister accepted the responsibility. Stefanie did not.

She rejected the idea that her generation must somehow share in the guilt. She objected to having to learn about Nazi horrors in school. "Enough that we Germans are always the bad ones," she fumed. "What does that mean—*we* started the war, *we* gassed the Jews, *we* devastated Russia. It sure as hell wasn't me. And no one in my class and none of my friends and certainly not my father. . . . They executed all the guilty ones back then at Nuremberg. . . . What do they want from me?"[6]

Her reaction, like a pebble in a pond, causes ripples that distort her views of the Holocaust in other ways. She looks at the Nazis as having been strong and glamorous figures who "looked great" in their uniforms.[7] She regards her Nazi grandfather as one who "sacrificed himself living and fighting for the fatherland, and the reward is a rope around his neck."[8] She disapproves of the idea of "restitution"—the German government giving Jews money to make up for what they have lost and what they have suffered.[9]

"Look at the Jews today," she sneers. "They say none survived. But today they're again all over the place. Do I know any personally? . . . How can I tell? Nowadays so many dark types are running around here: straight noses, crooked noses, Turks, Italians, Yugoslavs. How's one to tell who's a Jew and who isn't?"[10]

"Nicht Nazi!"

Stefanie is not a skinhead, or even a neo-Nazi, but it seems highly unlikely that she would do anything to stop such people from persecuting or physically abusing a person from a minority group. She and Rudolf are the extremes of their generations, the children and grandchildren of Germans who were adults during the Nazi years. They represent the opposite ends of the spectrum—deeply felt guilt and indignant rejection—of the feelings experienced by their peers. Most young Germans today position themselves somewhere toward the center of the area between those two positions.

Generally, today's young German people are less defensive about the Nazi atrocities than their parents were. That previous generation, which had to deal with the possibility of very real guilt on the part of their parents, came up with a variety of strategies to cushion the shock. Initially, those who had been children during and just after the Nazi era painted both Germans and Jews as figures in a much larger picture of anti-Semitism. "Not only Jews were victims, but also Gypsies and Communists," they pointed out. "Not only Germans were victimizers but also Ukrainians and the Allies."[11]

Shrugging off the six million Jewish dead, they would insist that "everybody is a victim of the Nazi regime." Not just the Germans, they would protest, but "all humans are capable of doing evil." As for any obligation to the Jews who survived, they would add that "everybody is a survivor of some sort." Viewing genocide as a universal sin, they would speak of the slaughter of Native Americans, and of the dropping of atomic bombs by the United States on Hiroshima and Nagasaki, killing hundreds of thousands of Japanese. Many denied personal involvement. *"Nicht Nazi!"* ("I am not a Nazi!") they would insist. "The Nazis did it, but nobody in my family was involved." And sometimes they claimed that the Holocaust had simply never happened. "There are no victims; we Germans were not involved."[12]

The majority of today's young Germans, a middle group that neither is tormented by guilt nor denies the Holocaust reality, mostly just show "signs of boredom and disinterest in Holocaust-related issues."[13] They regard the Holocaust much as the present generation of young Americans relates to the Great Depression of the 1930s. Such events are long ago and far away from personal experience.

The Holocaust seems ancient history to them.

COMING TO
TERMS WITH
HISTORY

8

I think that there is nothing wrong with visiting that cemetery [in Bitburg] where those young men [German soldiers] are victims of Nazism also. . . . They were victims, just as surely as the victims of the concentration camps.[1]

—President Ronald Reagan, April 18, 1985

hen former U.S. president Ronald Reagan announced that he planned to go to Bitburg, Germany, in May 1985 to "lay a wreath on the graves of Nazi SS soldiers," young Jews around the world were outraged.[2] To view the SS as equal victims of Nazism with Jews, they felt, was an insult to the millions slaughtered in the Holocaust, to their descendants, and to the few survivors. Young Jews took their lead from Holocaust survivor Elie Wiesel, who called the visit "a denial of the past,"[3] and who respectfully insisted, "That place, Mr. President, is not your place. Your place is with the victims of the SS."[4]

There may have been exceptions, but as a group, young Jews opposed the Bitburg visit. The reaction among young Germans—the grandchildren of Nazi-era Germans—was much more mixed. If the majority were hurt and puzzled by the negative Jewish reaction to what seemed a gesture to heal the wounds of a war that had been over for forty years, there was still a minority of young German people who spoke out against the ceremony.

These included members of religious youth groups from every denomination, the children of German union members (many unions opposed the visit on the grounds that when the Nazis were in power they had used the SS to suppress unions), young people who considered themselves left of center politically, and, of course, those few young Jews who are German citizens today. On the opposite side, there were young Germans who moved beyond resentment to insist that the Jewish reaction was an insult to the German nation. Some of them may have silently approved of the actions of skinheads and neo-Nazis who avenged the "insult" by vandalizing Jewish cemeteries and places of worship both before and after Reagan's visit.

Remembrance or Reconciliation?

Putting aside the extremists, the Bitburg incident is a clear example of how the lines are drawn for young people when they come to grips with the Holocaust. This does not mean just Germans and Jews, but for all young people who must consider an event in which millions of people, including children, were routinely slaughtered. If the Holocaust is not to be ignored, or its truth denied, then we must look carefully at the opposing views that emerged during the Bitburg controversy.

Call them the Jewish view and the German view. In the Jewish view, the Holocaust must never be forgotten. To let it fade from memory is to risk its happening again. To smooth over the past is to lose it. To honor the Nazi dead is to insult the Jewish victims. Part of never forgetting the Holocaust means never forgetting that it was Germans who brought it about.

Well-meaning young Germans are frustrated by the Jewish attitude. They feel that they have looked at the past and been horrified by it. They would make amends if they could. But it was a long time ago and they are individuals, not the state. Three generations past the Holocaust, there are those among them who are willing to take responsibility, but they don't know how. They feel guilty, but they do not want to feel guilty. Although they have done nothing themselves for which to be forgiven, they want forgiveness—if not for Germany, then at least for themselves.

The young Germans want reconciliation. The Jews want remembrance. Can it ever be possible to have both?

Dance of Anger; Dance of Hope

This was the question that was addressed in the winter of 1985 in Philadelphia when six young dancers formed the Jewish-German Dance Theatre. At first they concentrated on answering it among themselves. They were brutally honest. "I hate you for being German" were the words spoken directly to a German by a young Jew.[5] Similarly, resentment by Germans at the guilt being dumped on them by Jews was expressed openly. Allowing themselves to be angry with each other, the dancers worked out the movements to express that anger as well as routines to express the hope of getting past it. In this way they developed a full-length performance that they called *But What About the Holocaust?*

Their show toured several American cities. Then in October 1988 it went to Germany. It was so successful that it returned to Germany in June 1989.

Bjorn Krondorfer, one of the German cofounders of the group, has written about the German tours: "On stage we revealed our struggles with the past, with ourselves and each other, and with our cultures and families. Occasionally we involved the audience directly, albeit cautiously (for the staging of a production on the Holocaust by young American Jews and Germans in itself generated enough emotional turmoil). Often, Jewish survivors came to see our American performances. Many of them had avoided contact with Germans ever since their liberation. And when we performed in small rural towns in Germany, we often encountered audiences who had never before interacted with Jews."[6]

"Why Didn't the Jews Resist?"

It is true of younger Germans and Jews, particularly children and adolescents, that members of one group do not know any members of the other group and yet have strong opinions about them. Young Jews who have never met a German regard all Germans as brutal. Young Germans who have never met a Jew consider Jews victims by nature.

"Why didn't the Jews resist?" is a question asked frequently not just by German children, but by many other non-Jewish children.[7] The fact of armed Jewish resistance and of heroic daily struggles for survival somehow eludes them. They do not fully grasp the pressure of trying to make decisions that will be best for one's family when all the choices are bad ones, when flight is difficult if not impossible, when there is simply not enough money to buy survival for one's children. These young people have seen too many images of Jews being herded to the gas chambers. They may sincerely feel pity, but they find it hard to view Jews as anything but victims.

How Could Any German Not Know?

Most young Jews today—children, adolescents, and college students—do not view themselves as victims. They see themselves as descendants of martyrs and heroes. They draw courage from the past. They do not hesitate to ask the hard questions when it comes to Germans: Why did Germans choose a leader who had been preaching hatred of Jews for many years? Why did Germans do nothing when Jews were beaten in the streets, their shop windows broken, their homes and synagogues vandalized? Did they not notice when Jewish families were rounded up; herded into trucks; and shipped out, never to return? Did the children of neighbors, the children in school, not notice when their Jewish playmates disappeared? How is it possible that Germans could not have known about the death camps? That six million Jews could be killed and the secret kept from the German people?

Most of the young Jews who ask these questions are not seeking revenge. They do not want to punish the young Germans of today. At the same time, they do not consider it their job to relieve the guilt of the German nation. They hear the anguished answer of well-meaning young Germans—*"I wasn't even born yet!"*—but they are unmoved by it. Their priority is making sure that the Holocaust is never forgotten; coming to terms with the present generation of young Germans is not their main concern.

Facing Each Other

Is it hopeless then? Two groups, an ocean apart, did not think so, and in 1989 they acted. The Philadelphia Interfaith Council on the Holocaust and the Berlin *Evangelische Akademie* joined forces to design a four-week program involving young American Jews and non-Jewish Germans. African American, Asian American, and Native American students were also involved, as well as a young woman from the Netherlands and an Afghan student who lived in Germany.

All those in the group had volunteered with the understanding that they would spend two weeks in Philadelphia, with visits to New York and Washington, D.C., and two weeks in Berlin and Auschwitz. The idea was to confront the reality of the Holocaust, and the reality of their feelings about it and about Germans and Jews. They heard speakers on racism and anti-Semitism, as well as death-camp survivors. The hope was to reach an understanding in which both remembrance and reconciliation might be possible.

This was not easy. "We are not here to make anyone feel guilty," all of the speakers had assured the group.[8] Nevertheless, many of the Germans in the group did feel that there was a "'hidden agenda' . . . to make them feel guilty."[9] On the other hand, in Germany young Jews in the group were offended by being referred to as "*you* people" when they were accused of being oversensitive to language used by a local German historian talking about Jews.

"Operation Bitburg"

The group encounters demonstrated how young Germans and Jews tend to talk past one another, rather than to one another. Certain words that were flash-points of anger for one group were not recognized as such by the other. Opportunities for communication were missed by both sides.

Yet, slowly, a sort of understanding took form. The young Jews began to see how by characterizing Germans as a group rather than as individuals, they were taking a first step toward the very sort of bigotry that had led to the Holocaust.

One Jewish student came to recognize that "it doesn't seem to bother me as much to hear Jews tell their prejudices about Germans as it does to hear them talk about me. I'm not sure this is right."[10]

The German students gained an understanding of the depth of young Jews' feelings about the Holocaust. These were expressed strongly when Lucia, a German, spoke bitterly about how the parents of her Israeli boyfriend had pressured him to dump her by referring to their relationship as "operation Bitburg."[11] Four of the young Jews responded by saying they would never marry a non-Jewish person. The Germans saw this as prejudice against non-Jews. They were shocked and offended when the Jews implied that to marry a German would be to "give Hitler a posthumous victory."[12]

Curiosity and Hope

It took a while for the Germans to appreciate what the Jews meant by that and how deeply some of them felt about it. The Nazis had been bent on wiping out not just Jews but also Jewish culture, and they had almost succeeded. Intermarriage would seem to further weaken the Jewish heritage. The responsibility that many young Jews today felt that they owed to the dead of the Holocaust was to protect that heritage.

During any and all phases of the program, it would be a mistake to think that all Jews felt one way about an issue and all Germans another. There were Jews in the group who never saw anything wrong with intermarriage. There were Germans who felt that the Jews were right to try to preserve the purity of their culture.

All of the individuals in the group gained awareness from the program. In a sense they had youth on their side. Attitudes—particularly group loyalties and anti-group biases—harden over the years and create barriers between groups. The curiosity of young people can be a potent weapon in breaking down those barriers. This is true for all young people—not just Jews and Germans.

Overwhelming Holocaust Documentation

The majority of children in the United States today have no family connection to the Holocaust. To many it is indeed ancient history with no more immediate relevance to their lives than Hannibal crossing the Alps. To others, it seems an exaggeration of events that surely cannot have been as horrible as they are portrayed in film and story.

So-called revisionist historians have helped shape these attitudes by challenging the facts of the Holocaust. Some of them are motivated by a desire to relieve German guilt or to restore German pride. Some are trying to further a right-wing political agenda not only in Germany, but in other countries such as the United States as well. Some are quite simply neo-Nazis with Aryan, anti-Semitic, and white supremacist views. Regardless of motive, their efforts are, in part, responsible for recent polls finding that some 22 percent of Americans doubt that the Holocaust happened, or believe that the reports of the horrors and the statistics relating to them have been overstated. That figure may be even higher among young people.

The revisionists, however, cannot support their case. They cannot minimize the Holocaust. There is simply too much documentation and confirmed testimony that bear out the extent of the Holocaust. Six million Jews—men, women, and children—were murdered by the Nazis, along with members of other groups such as Gypsies, Russians, and Poles. Many of these victims were children.

The Death Books—carefully kept Nazi records of mass exterminations—testify to the genocide of those Hitler designated as *Untermenschen,* particularly Jews and Gypsies and their children. The Nazis preserved the paperwork that backs up these records. There are memos boasting of increases in exterminations, transportation records and schedules for the trains carrying victims to the death camps, signed orders authorizing medical experiments on children, bills for fuel for the crematoria, and receipts for the shipments of canisters of the gas that was pumped into the death chambers. There is also visual proof of the Holocaust. There are films taken by the Nazis of the murders. There are photographs snapped by individual Nazi soldiers, Ukrainian helpers, and others. There are pictures taken by the U.S. Army of American grave-digging machines digging pits to dispose of the bones of thousands of Holocaust victims. (At the end of the war, these remains constituted a health hazard.)

Forty-two volumes of war-crimes trial evidence provide testimony to the full extent of the Holocaust. Much of this evidence comes from eyewitnesses, many of them Germans.

The Need for Remembrance

The problem is that so much time has passed since the end of World War II and the Holocaust. Two generations of Americans have grown up since then, and a third is in grade school, middle school, and high school. It is only natural that the interests of young people should lie elsewhere. What does—what should—the Holocaust mean to them today?

Why is it so important that today's children understand the full extent of what happened to the children of the Holocaust? Perhaps the answer lies in the well-known belief that those who do not learn from the mistakes of history are doomed to repeat them. The Holocaust began with the Nazi theory that Aryan Germans were superior to other people. The result of this theory was the killing of more than 11 million people.

The Nazis were defeated, but their theory of superiority lives on in many forms. To some extent, almost all groups fall into the trap of believing themselves superior. Ethnic pride should be encouraged; it has many desirable aspects. But it can be a slippery slope leading to a mind-set that dehumanizes other groups. There are elements of this in conflicts around the world, such as those between the Serbs and the Croats, the Palestinians and the Israelis, the Turks and the Kurds, and the Tutsi and the Hutu. In the United States, these kinds of attitudes most often reveal themselves as racism. Learning about the Holocaust and how it came about, and understanding the horror to which it can lead, are the first steps in identifying those attitudes that may contain the seeds of future holocausts. Such understanding is the necessary first step in ensuring that genocide can never happen again.

The truth about the Holocaust must be received, understood, and passed along. Denying that truth is opening the door to future holocausts. Accepting it is how the children of today safeguard the children of tomorrow. The Holocaust was a tragedy for *all* children. All children must pledge that it shall never happen again.

CHRONOLOGY

1920–1929—Anti-Semitism builds in Germany.

1922—Ad in Nazi newspaper announces formation of the Hitler Youth.

1923–1924—Adolf Hitler writes *Mein Kampf.*

1926—The Hitler Youth is officially established as a unit of the Nazi party.

1933—January 30—Hitler comes to power as chancellor of Germany.

1933–1934—Official anti-Semitism affects Jewish children.

1935—September 15—Harsh anti-Semitic Nuremberg Laws are passed.

1938—March 14—German army invades Austria and is welcomed.

1938—November 9–10—*Kristallnacht*: Jewish shops vandalized; synagogues destroyed.

1939—September 1—World War II begins.

1941—July—Nazi government orders the "final solution of the Jewish question."

July 1941–March 1942—One million Jews are murdered, mostly by firing squads made up of SS troops, German Order Police, and non-German "helpers."

1942—January—Wannsee Conference is held to arrange carrying out "final solution" more efficiently.

1942–April 1945—Operation Reinhard—the mass killing of millions of Jews in concentration camp gas chambers is carried out.

1945—April—About 4,500 Hitler Youth die in the Battle of Berlin; the concentration camps are liberated; the war in Europe ends.

1945—August—President Truman receives report of ill treatment of Jews in displaced person camps; General Eisenhower orders reforms.

1946—At the newly formed United Nations, Eleanor Roosevelt successfully fights for refugees' right to have a choice about where to resettle.

1946—July—After sixty-one returning Jews are killed in Kielce, Poland, anti-Semitic riots occur in other towns throughout Eastern Europe.

1947—July—The *Exodus*, bound for Palestine with four thousand Jews aboard, is intercepted by the British and the Jews are sent back to Germany.

1948—May 15—The State of Israel is born. Arab armies attack Israel.

1979—November—First International Conference of Children of Holocaust Survivors is held in New York City.

1985—The Jewish-German Dance Theatre is formed in Philadelphia.

1985—May—Amid protests from Jews around the world, President Ronald Reagan lays a wreath on the grave of Nazi SS soldiers in Bitburg, Germany.

1987—*Born Guilty: Children of Nazi Families* by Peter Sichrovsky is published in Germany and provokes emotional reactions.

1988–1989—The Jewish-German Dance Theatre performs in Germany.

1989—The Philadelphia Interfaith Council on the Holocaust and the Berlin *Evangelische Akademie* design a four-week program focusing on encounters between young Germans and Jews.

CHAPTER NOTES

Introduction

1. Shalom Yoran, *The Defiant: A True Story* (New York: St. Martin's Press, 1996), p. 58.
2. United States Holocaust Memorial Museum brochure (Washington, DC: Children's Wall dedication, 1993).
3. Eileen Heyes, *Children of the Swastika: The Hitler Youth* (Brookfield, CT: Millbrook Press, 1993), p. 22. (Quoted from a March 1922 issue of the Nazi newspaper *Vöelkischer Beobachter*.)
4. Ibid., p. 57.
5. Joseph E. Persico, *Nuremberg: Infamy on Trial* (New York: Viking, 1994), p. 441.

Chapter One

1. Clifton Daniel, ed., *Chronicles of the 20th Century* (Mount Kisco, NY: Chronicle Publications, 1987), p. 295.
2. Daniel Jonah Goldhagen, *Hitler's Willing Executioners: Ordinary Germans and the Holocaust* (New York: Alfred A. Knopf, 1996), p. 82.
3. Ibid., p. 92.
4. Klaus P. Fischer, *Nazi Germany: A New History* (New York: Continuum, 1996), p. 385.
5. Ibid., p. 386.
6. Lucy S. Dawidowicz, *The War Against the Jews: 1933–1945* (New York: Holt, Rinehart and Winston, 1975), p. 58.

7. Fischer, p. 391.

8. Ibid.

9. Ibid., p. 392.

10. Dawidowicz, p. 100.

11. Fischer, p. 392.

12. Ibid.

13. Dawidowicz, p. 100.

Chapter Two

1. Claudia Koonz, *Mothers in the Fatherland: Women, the Family and Nazi Politics* (New York: St. Martin's Press, 1987), pp. 286–287.

2. *Encyclopaedia Britannica,* vol. 8 (Chicago: Encyclopaedia Britannica, Inc., 1984), p. 637.

3. Eileen Heyes, *Children of the Swastika: The Hitler Youth* (Brookfield, CT: Millbrook Press, 1993), pp. 35–36.

4. Ibid., pp. 35.

5. Klaus P. Fischer, *Nazi Germany: A New History* (New York: Continuum, 1996), p. 346.

6. Heyes, p. 57.

7. Ibid.

8. Fischer, p. 346.

9. Ibid., p. 347.

10. Ibid.

11. Ibid.

12. William L. Shirer, *The Rise and Fall of the Third Reich: A History of Nazi Germany* (New York: Simon & Schuster, 1960), p. 254.

13. Heyes, p. 61.

14. Ibid., p. 51.

15. Ibid., p. 36.

16. Ibid.

17. Ibid., p. 52.

18. Ibid., p. 64.

19. Ibid., p. 51.

Chapter Three

1. Maxine B. Rosenberg, *Hiding to Survive: Stories of Jewish Children Rescued From the Holocaust* (New York: Clarion Books, 1994), p. 117.
2. Ibid., p. 95.
3. Jeremy Josephs, *Swastika Over Paris: The Fate of the Jews in France* (New York: Little, Brown and Company, 1989), p. 40.
4. Deborah Dwork, *Children With a Star: Jewish Youth in Nazi Europe* (New Haven, CT: Yale University Press, 1991), p. 21.
5. Josephs, p. 70.
6. Ibid., p. 71.
7. Ibid., p. 167.
8. Howard Greenfeld, *The Hidden Children* (New York: Ticknor & Fields, 1993), p. 23.
9. Dwork, p. 105.
10. Andrew Handler and Susan V. Meschel, eds., *Young People Speak: Surviving the Holocaust in Hungary* (New York: Franklin Watts, 1993), p. 23.
11. Dwork, p. 80.
12. Ibid., p. 87.
13. Anne Frank, *The Diary of a Young Girl* (New York: Bantam Books, 1993), p. 277.
14. Ibid., pp. 211–212.
15. Ibid., p. 208.

Chapter Four

1. Jeremy Josephs, *Swastika Over Paris: The Fate of the Jews in France* (New York: Little, Brown and Company, 1989), p. 72.
2. Deborah Dwork, *Children With a Star: Jewish Youth in Nazi Europe* (New Haven, CT: Yale University Press, 1991), pp. 209–210.
3. William L. Shirer, *The Rise and Fall of the Third Reich: A History of Nazi Germany* (New York: Simon & Schuster, 1960), p. 964.
4. Daniel Jonah Goldhagen, *Hitler's Willing Executioners: Ordinary Germans and the Holocaust* (New York: Alfred A. Knopf, 1996), p. 149.

5. Elaine Landau, *We Survived the Holocaust* (Danbury, CT: Franklin Watts, 1991), p. 52.
6. Whitney R. Harris, *Tyranny on Trial: The Evidence at Nuremberg* (New York: Barnes & Noble Books, 1995), p. 306.
7. Dwork, p. xxxi.
8. Ibid., p. xxviii.
9. Ibid., p. 214.

Chapter Five

1. Martin Gilbert, *The Boys: Triumph Over Adversity* (London: Weidenfeld & Nicolson, 1996), pp. 242–243.
2. Azriel Eisenberg, *The Lost Generation: Children in the Holocaust* (New York: The Pilgrim Press, 1982), p. 292.
3. Ibid., p. 302.
4. Howard M. Sacher, *A History of the Jews in America* (New York: Alfred A. Knopf, 1992), p. 553.
5. Ibid., p. 555.
6. Paul Valent, *Child Survivors: Adults Living With Childhood Trauma* (Melbourne, Australia: William Heinemann Australia, 1993), p. 115.
7. Deborah Dwork, *Children With a Star: Jewish Youth in Nazi Europe* (New Haven, CT: Yale University Press, 1991), pp. 266–267.
8. Ibid., p. 267.
9. Joseph P. Lash, *Eleanor: The Years Alone* (New York: W. W. Norton & Company, Inc., 1972), pp. 51–52.
10. Valent, p. 115.
11. Judith S. Kestenberg and Eva Fogelman, eds., *Children During the Nazi Reign: Psychological Perspective on the Interview Process* (Westport, CT: Praeger, 1994), p. 165.
12. Valent, p. 115.
13. Gilbert, p. 244.
14. Ibid.

Chapter Six

1. Helen Epstein, *Children of the Holocaust: Conversations With Sons and Daughters of Survivors* (New York: Penguin Books, 1979), p. 31.

2. Bjorn Krondorfer, *Remembrance and Reconciliation: Encounters Between Young Jews and Germans* (New Haven, CT: Yale University Press, 1995), p. 76.

3. Ibid.

4. Gustav Niebuhr, "Painful Nazi Era Legacy," *The New York Times*, February 5, 1997, p. A8.

5. Ibid.

6. Steve Erlanger, "Albright Grateful for Her Parents' Painful Choices," *The New York Times*, February 5, 1997, p. A1.

7. Krondorfer, p. 54.

8. Art Spiegelman, *Maus II: A Survivor's Tale: And Here My Troubles Begin* (New York: Pantheon Books, 1991), p. 16.

9. Ibid., p. 44.

10. Art Spiegelman, *Maus: A Survivor's Tale: My Father Bleeds History* (New York: Pantheon Books, 1986), p. 97.

11. Epstein, p. 206.

12. Azriel Eisenberg, *The Lost Generation: Children in the Holocaust* (New York: Pilgrim Press, 1982), p. 325.

13. Ibid., p. 346.

14. Ibid.

15. Ibid., p. 345.

Chapter Seven

1. Peter Sichrovsky, *Born Guilty: Children of Nazi Families,* Trans. Jean Steinberg (New York: Basic Books, Inc., 1988), p. 22.

2. Klaus P. Fischer, *Nazi Germany: A New History* (New York: Continuum, 1996), p. 578.

3. Sichrovsky, p. 39.

4. Ibid., pp. 39–40.

5. Ibid., p. 47.

6. Ibid., p. 32.

7. Ibid., p. 30.
8. Ibid., p. 33.
9. Ibid., p. 34.
10. Ibid., pp. 32–33, 36.
11. Bjorn Krondorfer, *Remembrance and Reconciliation: Encounters Between Young Jews and Germans* (New Haven, CT: Yale University Press, 1995), p. 31.
12. Ibid., pp. 31–32.
13. Ibid., p. 24.

Chapter Eight

1. Bjorn Krondorfer, *Remembrance and Reconciliation: Encounters Between Young Jews and Germans* (New Haven, CT: Yale University Press, 1995), p. 23.
2. Clifton Daniel, ed., *Chronicles of the 20th Century* (Mount Kisco, NY: Chronicle Publications, 1987), p. 1257.
3. Ibid., p. 1258.
4. Krondorfer, p. 27.
5. Ibid., p. 6.
6. Ibid., pp. 6–7.
7. Ibid., p. 7.
8. Ibid., p. 65.
9. Ibid., p. 64.
10. Ibid., pp. 69–70.
11. Ibid., p. 66.
12. Ibid., p. 67.

GLOSSARY

anti-Semitism—irrational hatred and persecution of Jews

Aryans—supposed Indo-Iranian ancestors of Germans on whom Nazis based their master-race claims

Bund Deutscher Mädel (BDM)—Hitler Youth girls aged fifteen to eighteen

concentration camp—place of confinement for anti-Nazis and Jews; forced-labor place; slaughterhouse

Death Books—Nazi records of numbers of Jews killed each day in the camps

death camps—those concentration camps equipped for mass killing

Death's Head troops—SS units that guarded the concentration camps in Germany

fascist—one who believes in a system of government that imposes authoritarianism and militarism; name sometimes applied to Nazis

final solution—the Nazi plan to kill off the entire Jewish population of Europe

gas vans—trucks with sealed compartments used to murder victims by carbon monoxide fumes

genocide—the killing of a whole race, people, or nation

Germanization—the policy of populating occupied countries with pure-blooded Germans, particularly farmers

Gestapo—the Nazi secret police active in rounding up Jews for the death camps

ghetto—originally an area where Jews were forced to live

Hitler Youth—the organization that trained millions of German children and young people to fight for Nazi principles

Holocaust—systematic extermination of six million European Jews by the Nazis

Judenrein—free of Jews

Jungmädelbund (JM)—Hitler Youth girls aged ten to fourteen

Lebensraum—literally "room to live"; it was Hitler's policy of expanding Germany's borders through conquest

Mein Kampf (My Struggle)—Hitler's blend of autobiography and anti-Semitic call to arms

Pimpf—a boy aged ten to fourteen who belonged to the youngest division of the Hitler Youth

reconciliation—Jews and Germans coming to terms with each other and with the Holocaust

remembrance—determination by Jews not to let the Holocaust fade from memory

Schutzstaffel (SS)—Hitler's personal Nazi guard unit; expanded in the war to perform mass killings

shtetlach—small country villages populated by Jews (singular: shtetl)

slave laborers—Jewish, Polish, Czech, and other prisoners forced to work in German industry

Streifendienst—Hitler Youth group that spied on both children and adults

Sturmabteilung (SA)—Nazi storm troopers also known as "Brownshirts"

survivor guilt—emotion felt when someone close to you is killed, and you are not

synagogue—Jewish house of worship

Wannsee Conference—meeting of Nazi leaders in 1942 to plan how to kill Jews more efficiently

Weimar Republic—Germany between the end of World War I and the rise of Hitler

yellow star—a badge Nazis forced Jews to wear for ready identification

Zionist—one favoring the establishment of a Jewish nation

FOR MORE INFORMATION

Browning, Christopher R. *Ordinary Men: Reserve Police Battalion 101 and the Final Solution in Poland.* New York: HarperCollins Publishers, 1992.

Dwork, Deborah. *Children With a Star: Jewish Youth in Nazi Europe.* New Haven, CT: Yale University Press, 1991.

Eisenberg, Azriel. *The Lost Generation: Children in the Holocaust.* New York: The Pilgrim Press, 1982.

Frank, Anne. *Anne Frank: The Diary of a Young Girl.* New York: Pocket Books [paperback], 1953.

Gilbert, Martin. *The Boys: Triumph Over Adversity.* London: Weidenfeld & Nicolson, 1996.

Greenfeld, Howard. *The Hidden Children.* New York: Ticknor & Fields, 1993.

Handler, Andrew, and Susan V. Meschel. *Young People Speak: Surviving the Holocaust.* Danbury, CT: Franklin Watts, 1993.

Heyes, Eileen. *Children of the Swastika: The Hitler Youth.* Brookfield, CT: Millbrook Press, 1993.

Keneally, Thomas. *Schindler's List.* New York: Simon & Schuster, 1982.

Krondorfer, Bjorn. *Remembrance and Reconciliation: Encounters Between Young Jews and Germans.* New Haven, CT: Yale University Press, 1995.

Landau, Elaine. *We Survived the Holocaust.* Danbury, CT: Franklin Watts, 1991.

Persico, Joseph E. *Nuremberg: Infamy on Trial.* New York: Viking, 1994.

Rosenberg, Maxine B. *Hiding to Survive: Stories of Jewish Children Rescued From the Holocaust.* New York: Clarion Books, 1994.

Shirer, William L. *The Rise and Fall of the Third Reich: A History of Nazi Germany.* New York: Simon & Schuster, 1960.

Sichrovsky, Peter. *Born Guilty: Children of Nazi Families.* Trans. Jean Steinberg. New York: Basic Books, Inc., 1988.

Spiegelman, Art. *Maus: A Survivor's Tale: My Father Bleeds History.* New York, Pantheon Books [paper], 1986.

Spiegelman, Art. *Maus II: A Survivor's Tale: And Here My Troubles Begin.* New York, Pantheon Books, 1991.

Yoran, Shalom. *The Defiant: A True Story.* New York: St. Martin's Press, 1996.

Internet Sites

(All have links to related sites.)

The United States Holocaust Memorial Museum
www.ushmm.org

The Holocaust: An Historical Summary
www.ushmm.org/education/history.html

Holocaust Resources on the World Wide Web
www.fred.net/nhhs/html/hololink.htm

The Jewish Student Online Research Center (JSOURCE)
www.us-israel.org/jsource/

Remembering the Holocaust
yarra.vicnet.net.au/~aragorn/holocaus.htm

INDEX